DK EYEWITNESS

TOP 1

SAN DIEGO

T0046992

Top 10 San Diego Highlights

The Top 10 of Everything

CONTENTS

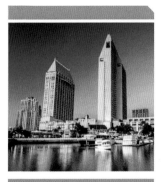

San Diego Area by Area

Streetsmart

Within each Top 10 list in this book, no hierarchy of quality or popularity is implied. All 10 are, in the editor's opinion, of roughly equal merit.
   Throughout this book, floors are referred to in accordance with American usage; i.e., the "first floor" is at ground level.

Title page, front cover and spine *Aerial view of the Pacific Beach and Mission Bay*
Back cover, clockwise from top left *Mission Basilica San Diego de Alcalá; La Jolla coastline; Balboa Park; Pacific Beach and Mission Bay; Gaslamp Quarter sign in Downtown San Diego*

The rapid rate at which the world is changing is constantly keeping the DK Eyewitness team on our toes. While we've worked hard to ensure that this edition of San Diego is accurate and up-to-date, we know that opening hours alter, standards shift, prices fluctuate, places close and new ones pop up in their stead. So, if you notice we've got something wrong or left something out, we want to hear about it. Please get in touch at **travelguides@dk.com**

Welcome to
San Diego

San Diego is the riviera of North America, pure and simple, with long stretches of spectacular sandy beaches. The birthplace of the state of California is also historic, hip, active, and friendly, bestowing a warm welcome upon everyone who comes here. With DK Eyewitness Top 10 San Diego, it's yours to explore.

San Diego boasts ritzy villages, retro surf towns, and movie-star good looks, with a cornucopia of gasp-worthy views, from the colorful flotilla of **San Diego Bay**, to the lush city of **La Jolla** to the north. It is also one of the few places on earth where you can flit from ocean to mountains to desert and back to the city in the span of an afternoon. It is easy to see why San Diegans are proud of **Balboa Park**, with its showcase gardens and excellent museums. This is where locals keep fit, laze, dream, and play. And they do love to play, enjoying Comic-Con International, as well as festivals and outdoor concerts.

The city has all the advantages of a big city, minus the bustle, and a mild climate year-round. A stroll along the **Embarcadero** takes you from the historic *Star of India* tall ship, past the modern cruise terminal, all the way to the formidable **USS *Midway*** aircraft carrier. The historic **Gaslamp Quarter**, once home to bawdy houses, dance halls, and gambling saloons, is now full of popular shops, bars, and nightclubs. A number of original buildings have become superstar hotels and restaurants.

Whether you're visiting for a weekend or a week, our Top 10 guide brings together the best of everything the city has to offer. The guide has useful tips throughout, from seeking out what's free to finding the best beaches, plus six easy-to-follow itineraries, designed to tie together a clutch of sights in a short space of time. Add inspiring photography and detailed maps, and you've got the essential pocket-sized travel companion. **Enjoy the book, and enjoy San Diego**.

Clockwise from top: Spanish Village Art Center at Balboa Park, Scripps Pier in La Jolla, La Jolla Cove, exterior of the Mormon Temple, the San Diego Museum of Art, marina with a view of downtown San Diego, Balboa Park in the evening

Exploring San Diego

A San Diego visit can hop from historic sights to sunny beaches to snowcapped mountains to exotic desert – and then back downtown in time for dinner. There is a wealth of things to see and do, and the city caters to all interests. These two- and four-day itineraries will help you plan your time and make the most of your visit to the city.

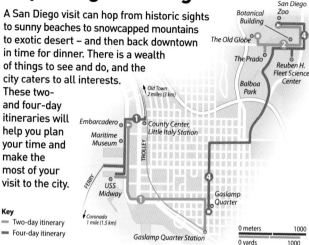

Key
— Two-day itinerary
━ Four-day itinerary

Two Days in San Diego

Day ❶
MORNING

Awaken to a view of the bay and then take a morning stroll along the **Embarcadero** (see pp14–15). Check out the vessels at the **Maritime Museum** (see p47), and board the behemoth **USS Midway** (see pp16–17).

AFTERNOON

Wander the historic **Gaslamp Quarter** (see pp12–13) on a self-guided or organized tour, then trolley to the **Old Town State Historic Park** (see pp24–5) and immerse yourself in early Californian life. Cap off the day at the **Mission Basilica San Diego de Alcalá** (see pp30–31), before heading back to the coast to watch the sun set.

Day ❷
MORNING

Start off at the **San Diego Zoo** (see p19), touring by foot or tram, then explore the rest of **Balboa Park** (see pp18–19). Browse Spanish Village artisan shops along the way.

AFTERNOON

Visit one or more of San Diego's renowned museums and galleries (see pp46–7); many of them have cafés for lunch. Rest your feet at the **Botanical Building** (see p18) and lily pond, where buskers perform nearby. Make advance reservations for dinner at **The Prado at Balboa Park** (see pp66–7), and catch a show at **The Old Globe** (see p60).

Four Days in San Diego

Day ❶
MORNING

Begin your day at **Old Town State Historic Park** (see pp24–5), venturing out of the park to **Whaley House Museum** (see p86) and **Presidio Park** (see p86). Shop for trinkets at **Bazaar del Mundo** (see p88), then lunch at **Old Town Mexican Café & Cantina** (see p89).

AFTERNOON

Trolley to the **Mission Basilica San Diego de Alcalá** (see pp30–31), then head to the **Embarcadero** (see pp14–15). Soak up the city's nautical heritage at the **Maritime Museum** (see p47) or **USS Midway** (see pp16–17). Catch the ferry to **Coronado** (see pp26–7) for sunset cocktails at the **Hotel del Coronado** (see p44).

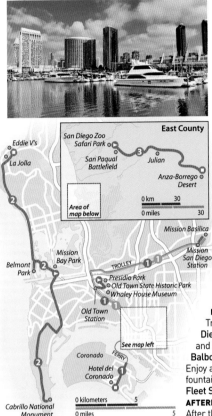

Embarcadero, the waterfront area, has been the heart of San Diego since the mid-1500s.

Day ❸

MORNING

Head northeast to **San Diego Zoo Safari Park** *(see p59)*. Continue past **San Pasqual Battlefield** *(see p43)* up the mountain to **Julian** *(see p42)*.

AFTERNOON

Have lunch on Julian's Main Street, pan for gold at Eagle Mine, and shop for local crafts. Drop down to the **Anza-Borrego Desert State Park** *(see p37)* at twilight. Native American casinos *(see p56)* may tempt you on the way back to downtown San Diego.

Day ❹

MORNING

Tram through the **San Diego Zoo** *(see p19)* and head for the sights of **Balboa Park** *(see pp18–19)*. Enjoy a picnic lunch by the fountain outside **Reuben H. Fleet Science Center** *(see p59)*.

AFTERNOON

After the park, enjoy dinner and a music club in the historic **Gaslamp Quarter** *(see pp12–13)*, ending the day in the lively bars.

Day ❷

MORNING

Lazy beaches and lots of water- and land-based sports await visitors at **Mission Bay Park** *(see pp32–3)*. Take a spin on the 1925 Giant Dipper roller coaster at **Belmont Park** *(see p33)*.

AFTERNOON

Journey to the **Cabrillo National Monument** *(see p80)*. Explore tide pools and the lighthouse, and gaze over the busy bay from the visitor center. Continue up the coast to **La Jolla** *(see p34–5)* to enjoy its chic shops, classy restaurants, and illustrious beaches. See the sun set over La Jolla Cove from **Eddie V's** *(see p67)* upstairs patio, with live jazz.

Gaslamp Quarter's famous overhead signage at the beginning of 5th Avenue, acts as a landmark.

Top 10 San Diego Highlights

The idyllic beach at the waterfront
area of Embarcadero

🔟 San Diego Highlights

With a sunny climate and a splendid setting along the Pacific, San Diegans live the California Dream. A vibrant downtown area and world-class attractions keep the city's spirit young, but its heart lies in its beginnings as the birthplace of California.

1 Gaslamp Quarter

Old wrought-iron gas lamps lead the way to the hottest scene in town. Rocking nightspots and vibrant restaurants give life to San Diego's historic downtown area (see pp12–13).

2 Embarcadero

With its nautical museums, vintage ships, and superb views across the harbor, the Embarcadero links the city to its ocean heritage (see pp14–17).

3 Balboa Park

San Diegans take pride in having one of the finest urban parks in the world. Its famous zoo, fascinating museums, and exquisite gardens offer endless activities (see pp18–21).

4 Old Town State Historic Park

In this, the original center of San Diego, adobe houses, wood-framed buildings, and early artifacts have been restored (see pp24–5).

5 Coronado

This idyllic community is famous for the Hotel del Coronado. Coronado's white sandy beaches, sidewalk cafés, and oceanfront mansions have enticed visitors for over a century (see pp26–7).

6 Point Loma
In 1542, Juan Cabrillo arrived at Ballast Point, claiming California for Spain. Now, stunning homes and marinas grace Point Loma's waterfront *(see pp28–9)*.

Mission Basilica San Diego de Alcalá 7
Saint Junípero Serra established this mission in 1769 to Christianize the Native Americans *(see pp30–31)*.

8 Mission Bay Park
This aquatic wonderland epitomizes San Diego's laid-back lifestyle, from its watersports to the paths for cycling and strolling *(see pp32–3)*.

9 La Jolla
This exclusive community is noted for the Scripps Institution of Oceanography, a world-renowned research facility *(see pp34–5)*.

10 East County
About an hour east of the city, you can ride a vintage train, hike the forest, pan for gold, climb a mountain, and stargaze in the desert *(see pp36–7)*.

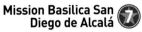

🔟⭐ Gaslamp Quarter

Great nightclubs, trendy restaurants, and unique boutiques compete for attention in San Diego's most vibrant neighborhood. Alonzo Horton's 1867 New Town seemed doomed to the wrecking ball in the 1970s, but a civic revitalization program transformed the dilapidated area into a showcase destination. By 1980, the Gaslamp Quarter was decreed a National Historic District.

1 Ingle Building

A mural marks the Golden Lion Tavern that was once located here. Note the lion sculptures, stained-glass windows, and 1906 stained-glass dome over the bar.

NEED TO KNOW

MAP J5 » www.gaslamp.org

Ingle Building: 801 4th St

San Diego Hardware: 840 5th Ave

William Heath Davis House: 410 Island Ave 619 233 4692; open 10am–5pm Tue–Sat, noon–4pm Sun; adm $10

Louis Bank of Commerce: 835 5th Ave

Keating Building: 432 F St

Lincoln Hotel: 536 5th Ave

Balboa Theatre: 868 4th Ave

Old City Hall: 664 5th Ave

Yuma Building: 643 5th Ave

■ Stop at the Ghirardelli Chocolate Shop *(643 5th Ave)* for a hot fudge sundae.

■ Parking is difficult on weekends. Take the San Diego Trolley; it stops right at Gaslamp.

■ Historical walking tours are held 1pm Thu & 11am Sat *($25; www.gaslampfoundation.org).*

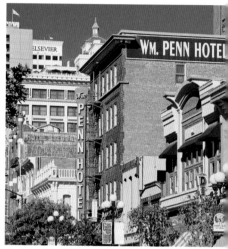

The historic buildings of the Gaslamp Quarter

2 San Diego Hardware

Once a dance hall, then a five-and-dime store, this building housed one of San Diego's oldest businesses, founded in 1892. Though the store relocated in 2006, the original storefront remains on Fifth Avenue.

3 William Heath Davis House

Named after the man who tried but failed to develop San Diego in 1850, the museum is home to the Gaslamp Quarter Historical Foundation. It's the oldest wooden structure in the downtown area.

4 Louis Bank of Commerce

A bank until 1893, this Victorian structure **(below)** was the favorite bar of Wyatt Earp *(see p41)*. It once contained the Golden Poppy Hotel, a notorious brothel.

6 Keating Building

Fannie Keating built this Romanesque-style building **(left)** in 1890 in honor of her husband George. It once housed some of the most prestigious offices in the whole town.

7 Lincoln Hotel

Built in 1913, the four-story hotel features Chinese elements, the original beveled glass in its upper stories, and its original green-and-white ceramic tile facade. Japanese prisoners were housed here before they were forcibly removed to internment camps during World War II.

STINGAREE DISTRICT

After its legitimate businesses relocated in the late 19th century, New Town was home to brothels, opium dens, saloons, and gambling halls, some operated by famous lawman Wyatt Earp. It became known as "Stingaree" because one could be stung on its streets as easily as by the sting-aree fish in the bay. After police tried (and failed) to clean up Stingaree in 1912, it slowly disintegrated into a slum until rescued by the Gaslamp Quarter Foundation some 50 years later.

Gaslamp Quarter Map

5 Wrought-Iron Gas Lamps

San Diego's historic district is named after the quaint green wrought-iron gas lamps that line the streets – they actually run on electricity.

8 Balboa Theatre

This landmark 1,500-seat theater **(above)** started out as a grand cinema with waterfalls flanking the stage. Notice the beautiful tiled dome on the roof. A restoration project converted the building into a venue for live performances (see p60).

9 Old City Hall

Dating from 1874, this Italianate building features 16-ft (5-m) ceilings, brick arches, Classical columns, and a wrought-iron cage elevator. In 1900, the entire city government could fit inside. Today, the building houses condos, shops, and a restaurant.

10 Yuma Building

Captain Wilcox of the US *Invincible* owned downtown's first brick structure in 1888. The building was named for his business dealings in Yuma, Arizona. Airy residential lofts with large bay windows now occupy the upper levels of the building.

𝐓𝐎𝐏𝟏𝟎 ⭐ **Embarcadero**

Ever since Juan Cabrillo sailed into San Diego Bay in 1542, much of the city's life has revolved around its waterfront. Settlers stepped ashore on its banks; immigrants worked as whalers and fishermen; the US Navy left an indelible mark with its shipyards and warships. Tourism has added another layer to the harbor's lively atmosphere. The Embarcadero welcomes visitors with its art displays, walkways, nautical museums, harbor cruises, and benches on which to sit and enjoy the uninterrupted harbor activity.

① San Diego Harbor

One of the greatest attractions of the Embarcadero is this bustling harbor **(above)**, where you can watch Navy destroyers, aircraft carriers, ferries, cruise ships, and sailboats glide past. Be a part of the action by taking a harbor cruise.

③ San Diego County Administration Center

Dedicated by President F. Roosevelt, this 1936 civic structure (see p44) looks especially magisterial at night. Enter through the west door and feel free to wander about.

④ Tuna Harbor

San Diego was once home to the world's largest tuna fleet, with 200 commercial boats. Portuguese immigrants dominated the trade until the canneries moved to Mexico and Samoa. The US Tuna Foundation still keeps its offices here.

Seaport Village ②

New England and Spanish design **(right)** blend eclectically in this waterfront area (see p69) with brilliant harbor views.

Embarcadero Map

SAN DIEGO AND THE MILITARY

San Diego has had strong military ties ever since the Spanish built the presidio (fortress) in 1769, and the military contributes handsomely to the local economy. Their presence is everywhere: Navy SEALS train at Coronado, three aircraft carriers and warships berth in the harbor, and Marines land amphibious tanks along Camp Pendleton. Ship parades and tours are popular events in San Diego's September/October Fleet Week.

⑦ San Diego Convention Center

The center **(above)** was designed to complement the waterfront location, with its flying buttresses, skylight tubes, and rooftop sails.

⑧ Piers

Glistening cruise ships bound for Mexico and the Panama Canal tie up at B Street Pier. Harbor cruises and ferries to Coronado can be caught nearby.

⑨ Santa Fe Depot

The train cars may be modern, but the atmosphere recalls the stylish days of rail travel. The interiors of the Spanish-Colonial style building feature burnished oak benches, original tiles, and chandeliers.

⑩ Maritime Museum of San Diego

Nautical lovers can gaze at *San Salvador*, *Star of India*, *Berkeley* **(below)**, *Medea*, and other vintage ships *(see p47)* restored to their former glory.

⑤ USS Midway Museum

The 1,000-ft (305-m) USS *Midway (see pp16–17)*, commissioned in 1945, was once the world's largest warship. Many docents on board are veterans of the carrier.

⑥ Embarcadero Marina Park

Relax on one of the grassy expanses to enjoy the excellent views of the harbor and Coronado Bridge. Joggers and bicyclists use the paths around the park *(see p53)*, and on weekends, entertainers and artists demonstrate their work.

NEED TO KNOW
MAP J6

USS Midway Museum: 910 N. Harbor Dr; 619 544 9600; open 10am–4pm daily; adm adult $26, child $18

Santa Fe Depot: 1050 Kettner Blvd

■ Flagship Cruises *(see p114)* offers 1- and 2-hour narrated tours. There are several departures daily.

■ For a quick bite, try Hazelwood's On The Bay *(1355 N Harbor Dr)*. Their fresh sandwiches are good outdoor options.

■ Pedicabs are usually available to take you down to Seaport Village.

USS Midway Museum

1 **Hangar Deck**
The hangar deck stored the carrier's aircraft, with elevators raising planes up to the flight deck as needed. Now the carrier's entry level, it has audio-tour headsets, aircraft displays, a gift shop, café, and restrooms. Don't miss the 24-ft (7-m) Plexiglas model of the *Midway* used in World War II to construct the carrier.

USS Midway Museum Floor Plan

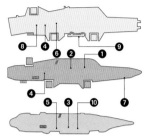

Key to Floor Plan
- Roof Flight Deck and Island
- Hangar Deck and Forecastle
- 2nd, 3rd, and 4th Decks

Fighter plane on the hangar deck

2 **Virtual Reality Flight Simulations**
For an additional price, which also includes a briefing, a flight suit, and 30 minutes of flight, you can experience flying a plane by taking the controls of a flight simulator. Also on hand are several standard flight stations, where, for another ticket, you can practice taking off from a carrier.

3 **Post Office**
The *Midway*'s crew often had to wait several weeks at a time for a Carrier Onboard Delivery flight to receive letters from home. The post office was also in charge of the disbursement of money orders.

4 **Aircraft**
More than two dozen planes and helicopters are on display on the flight and hangar decks. Among the

displays are the F-14A Tomcat, which flies at speeds exceeding Mach 2, two F-4 Phantoms, and an A-6E Intruder. The *Midway* once held up to 80 aircraft.

5 **Galley**
The *Midway* could store up to 1.5-million lbs (680,388 kg) of dry provisions and a quarter-million lbs (113,398 kg) of meat and vegetables to serve the crew 13,000 meals daily.

6 **Flight Deck**
The area of the *Midway*'s flight deck is roughly 4 acres (1.6 ha) in size. Additional aircraft are displayed here, and the Island is entered from here. The flight deck was where dramatic landings and take-offs took place – take-offs were from the bow, and the angled deck was used for landings.

Flight deck of the USS *Midway*

HISTORY OF THE MIDWAY

Commissioned on September 10, 1945, the *Midway* was named after the Battle of Midway, which was the turning point for the Allies in the War of the Pacific. It remained the largest ship in the world for ten years, and was the first ship too large to transit the Panama Canal. After participating in the Vietnam War, it saw further action during Operation Desert Storm in 1991, and finished its years of service by evacuating military personnel threatened by the 1991 eruption of Mount Pinatubo in the Philippines. The *Midway* was decommissioned in 1992.

TOP 10 MIDWAY STATISTICS

1 Overall length: 1,001 ft, 6 inches (305 m)

2 Width: 258 ft (78.6 m)

3 Height: 222 ft, 3 inches (67.7 m)

4 Full displacement: 70,000 tons (63,502,932 kg)

5 Number of propellers: 4

6 Weight of each propeller: 22 tons (19,958 kg)

7 Boilers: 12

8 Miles of piping: 200 (322 km)

9 Miles of copper conductor: 3,000 (4,828 km)

10 Ship fuel capacity: 2.23 million gallons (8.4 million liters)

Vietnam War anniversary gathering, USS *Midway*

 Berths
Sleeping berths for 400 of the 4,500 crew members are displayed on the hangar deck. Beds were too short to be comfortable for anyone over 6 ft (1.8 m), and the accompanying metal lockers could hold barely more than a uniform. Enlisted men were often just out of high school.

8 Arresting Wire and Catapults
Notice the arresting wire on the flight deck. This enabled a pilot to land a 20-ton jet cruising at 150 miles (241 km) an hour on an area the size of a tennis court. A hook attached to the tail of a plane grabbed the wire during landing. Two steam catapults helped propel the plane for take-off.

9 Island
Ladders take you up to the navigation room and bridge, sometimes called the Superstructure, from where the ship's movements were commanded. The flight control deck oversaw aircraft operations.

The Island, or Superstructure

10 Metal Shop
On the mess deck, the metal shop produced metal structures and replicated metal parts for the ship or its aircraft. Self-sufficiency and versatility were the keywords for tours of duty when the ship would be away for months at a time.

🔟 ⭐ Balboa Park

Since the early 20th century, Balboa Park has awed San Diegans with its romantic hillside setting, lush landscaping, and splendid architecture. The park's magnificent Spanish structures date from the 1915–16 Panama-California Exposition. On weekends, thousands of visitors come to indulge their interests, whether it's recreational, Shakespeare, or art. However, the park is probably best known for being home to a wealth of excellent museums as well as the world-famous San Diego Zoo.

2 Botanical Building

Constructed for the 1915–16 Panama-California Exposition, the Botanical Building is one of the world's largest lath structures. It houses more than 2,100 orchids, palms, and other tropical plants, and seasonal flowers.

1 Reuben H. Fleet Science Center

Explore sense and touch **(above)** in the Gallery of Illusions and Perceptions *(see p59)*, learn about electricity, digital recording, and tornados, or catch an IMAX movie or a planetarium show.

3 The Old Globe

The Tony-winning Old Globe Theatre, the Sheryl and Harvey White Theatre, and the Lowell Davies Festival Theatre form a wonderful cultural resource *(see p60)*.

BALBOA PARK AND WORLD WAR II

More than 2,000 beds were lined up in Balboa Park's museums for those wounded in 1941's Pearl Harbor attack. All buildings were used for barracks. The park became one of the largest hospital training centers in the world: 600 Navy nurses were stationed at the House of Hospitality, and the lily pond served as a rehab pool. In 1947, the military returned the park to the city.

4 Casa del Prado

The outstanding structure is a reconstruction of a building from the Panama-California Exposition. Wall reliefs commemorate Saint Junípero Serra and Juan Cabrillo.

5 Spanish Village Art Center

Architect Richard Requa *(see p41)* wanted visitors to experience the simple life of a Spanish village **(above)**. This complex *(see p47)* houses 37 art and craft studios.

6 House of Hospitality
Modeled on a hospital in Spain and now a visitor center, this was erected for the Panama-California Exposition and rebuilt in the 1990s.

7 House of Pacific Relations
Founded in 1935, these cottages feature cultural ambassadors from 33 countries showcasing local traditions.

Balboa Park Map

10 California Tower and Dome
Built for the Exposition, this building **(below)**, with its 200-ft (61-m) tower, has come to represent San Diego's identity. Famous figures of the city's past are represented on the facade. Inside is the Museum of Us *(see p20)*.

8 Spreckels Organ Pavilion
One of the world's largest outdoor organs, it contains 4,530 pipes **(above)**. The metal curtain protecting it weighs close to 12 tons. Free recitals are held on Sundays.

9 San Diego Zoo
In this zoo, almost 4,000 animals and 800 species reside in re-created natural habitats. Thanks to breeding programs and webcams, threatened baby koalas are now superstars.

NEED TO KNOW

MAP L2 ■ www.balboa park.org

Botanical Building: open 10am–4pm Fri–Wed

House of Hospitality: open 9:30am–5pm daily

House of Pacific Relations: open 11am–5pm Sat & Sun

Spreckels Organ Pavilion: regular concerts: 2–3pm Sun; summer concerts: 7:30–9pm Mon (mid-Jun–Aug)

San Diego Zoo: open 9am–6pm (to 9pm Jun 24–Sep 4); adm adult $62, child $52

■ An annual, parkwide, or limited explorer pass can be purchased at the visitor center as per requirement.

■ Get lunch at the Japanese Sculpture Garden's Tea Pavilion.

■ Some parking lots aren't open until 8:30am.

Balboa Park Museums

① San Diego Museum of Us

MAP L1 ▪ 619 239 2001 ▪ Open 10am–5pm Wed–Sun ▪ Adm ▪ www.museumofus.org

Learn about evolution from a replica of a 4-million-year-old human ancestor, and visit the Ancient Egypt room for mummies and funerary objects. Artifacts from the Kumeyaay, San Diego's original inhabitants, and a replica of a Mayan monument emphasize the culture of the Americas.

② San Diego Museum of Art

MAP L1 ▪ 619 232 7931 ▪ Open 10am–5pm Thu–Tue, noon–5pm Sun ▪ Adm ▪ www.sdmart.org

This exceptional museum has works by old masters and major 19th- and 20th-century artists. Be sure to check out the Asian art collection.

Visitors at San Diego Museum of Art

③ Mingei International Museum

MAP L1 ▪ 619 239 0003 ▪ Open 10am–5pm Tue–Thu & Sun (to 6pm Fri & Sat) ▪ Adm ▪ www.mingei.org

The Japanese word *mingei* means "art of the people" and on view here is a display of international folk art. Exhibits include textiles, jewelry, furniture, and pottery.

Display at the Natural History Museum

④ San Diego Natural History Museum

MAP M1 ▪ 619 232 3821 ▪ Open 10am–4pm Fri–Tue ▪ Adm ▪ www.sdnhm.org

Galleries showcase the evolution and diversity of California. Exhibits, guided weekend nature walks, and field trips explore the natural world.

⑤ Timken Museum of Art

MAP L1 ▪ 619 239 5548 ▪ Open 10am–4:30pm Tue–Sun (from noon Sun) ▪ www.timkenmuseum.org

The collection includes Rembrandt's *Saint Bartholomew*, and works by Rubens and Bruegel the Elder.

⑥ San Diego History Center

MAP L1 ▪ 619 232 6203 ▪ Open 11am–4pm Fri–Sun ▪ Adm ▪ www.sandiegohistory.org

An alternating collection of old photographs and artifacts that introduce San Diego's early years.

⑦ Museum of Photographic Arts

MAP L1 ▪ 619 238 7559 ▪ Open 11am–4pm Thu–Sun ▪ Adm ▪ www.mopa.org

Temporary exhibitions featuring the world's most celebrated camera geniuses mix with pieces from the museum's permanent collection. The theater screens film classics.

8 San Diego Air and Space Museum

MAP L2 ▪ 619 234 8291
▪ Open 10am–4:30pm daily ▪ Adm
▪ www.sandiegoairandspace.org

One of the museum's finest planes, the Lockheed A-12 Blackbird spy plane, greets you on arrival. Don't miss the International Aerospace Hall of Fame.

Balboa Park Museums Map

9 San Diego Automotive Museum

MAP L2 ▪ 619 231 2886 ▪ Open 11am–5pm Tue–Fri, 10am–5pm Sat–Sun ▪ Adm ▪ www. sdautomuseum.org

Discover California's car culture through classic vehicles and fascinating exhibits. A Racing Hall of Fame honors past giants of the racing world.

A classic car at San Diego Automotive Museum

10 Centro Cultural de la Raza

MAP L2 ▪ 619 363 1372 ▪ Open noon–4pm Tue–Sun ▪ www. centrodelaraza.com

This former water tower, decorated with colorful murals, celebrates indigenous, Chicano, Mexican, and Latino art and culture with rotating exhibits and performances.

THE MOTHER OF BALBOA PARK

Horticulturalist Kate Sessions needed room to establish a nursery in 1910. She struck a deal with the city of San Diego in which she promised to plant 100 trees a year in the then-called City Park and 300 trees elsewhere in exchange for 36 acres. A 35-year planting frenzy resulted in 10,000 glorious trees and shrubs, shady arbors draped with bougainvillea, and flower gardens that burst with color throughout the year.

**TOP 10
GARDENS OF BALBOA PARK**

1 Alcázar Gardens
2 Japanese Friendship Garden
3 Botanical Building and Lily Ponds
4 Palm Canyon
5 Casa del Rey Moro
6 Zoro Garden
7 Rose Garden
8 Desert Garden
9 Florida Canyon
10 Moreton Bay Fig Tree

The Alcázar Gardens look particularly beautiful and colorful when in full bloom during the spring.

Following pages The striking San Diego bay and skyline

TOP 10 ⭐ Old Town State Historic Park

After Mexico won its independence from Spain in 1821, many retired soldiers created what is now Old Town, laying their homes and businesses around the plaza in typical Spanish style. Through trade with Boston, the town began to prosper. After a fire in 1872 destroyed much of the commercial center, San Diego moved to a "New Town" closer to the bay. Today, you can explore the preserved and restored structures of San Diego's settler families.

1 Plaza
The plaza was once used by Spanish communities for bull-fights, political events, executions, and fiestas. Since 1846, tradition maintains that the Old Town flagpole must be made from a ship's mast.

La Casa de Estudillo 2
Built in 1827 by José Estudillo, the Presidio's commander, this adobe home **(right)** is Old Town's show-piece. Workmen shaped the curved red tiles of the roof by spreading clay over their legs.

3 Seeley Stable Museum
Before railroads, Albert Seeley ran a stagecoach business between San Diego and LA. This barn **(below)** houses original carriages and wagons from the Wild West.

4 Mason Street School
This one-room school opened in 1865. Its first teacher, Mary Chase Walker, resigned her $65-a-month position when townspeople complained that she had invited a Black woman to lunch.

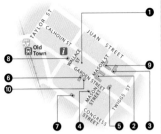

Old Town State Historic Park Map

FIRST IMPRESSIONS

In his epic story of early San Diego, *Two Years Before the Mast* (1840), Richard Henry Dana described the town as "a small settlement directly before the fort, composed of about 40 dark-brown-looking huts or houses, and two larger ones plastered." Bostonian Mary Chase Walker, San Diego's first schoolhouse teacher, was more blunt: "Of all the dilapidated, miserable looking places I had ever seen, this was the worst."

5 San Diego Union Historical Museum

This wood-frame house was built in New England and shipped down in 1851. It was home to the early years of *The San Diego Union*, the city's oldest newspaper.

7 La Casa de Machado y Stewart

Jack Stewart married Rosa Machado in 1845 and moved to this adobe home, where the family remained until 1966. It was restored by California State Parks.

8 Robinson-Rose House

Docents are on hand to answer questions at this house, which dates from 1853 and is the headquarters of Old Town. Look out for the model of the 1872 Old Town.

9 La Casa de Bandini

Peruvian Juan Bandini arrived in San Diego in 1819 and became one of its wealthiest citizens. His former home (below) is now the Cosmopolitan Hotel.

6 Colorado House

The name Wells Fargo came to symbolize the opening of the American West. At this little museum housed in a former hotel (above), a restored stagecoach is the main exhibit.

NEED TO KNOW

MAP N5 ▪ 4002 Wallace St ▪ 619 220 5422 ▪ www.parks.ca.gov

Open May–Sep: 10am–5pm daily; Oct–Apr: 10am–4:30pm daily

La Casa de Estudillo: closed Mon

Seeley Stable Museum: closed Tue

▪ Head to one of San Diego's most famous Mexican restaurants, Old Town Mexican Café & Cantina *(see p89)*, and watch the chefs make tortillas as you have lunch.

▪ One-hour walking tours led by park staff leave daily at 11am and 2pm from the Robinson-Rose House.

▪ Park concessionaires sell traditional souvenirs and other wares; nearby Bazaar del Mundo offers colorful, unique items.

10 First San Diego Courthouse

This reconstruction of the 1847 courthouse marks the city's first fire-brick structure. Not to be missed is the ominous 1860 jail cell out back.

Coronado

Sometimes described as an island because its village-like atmosphere is far removed from the big city, picturesque Coronado lies on a sliver of land between the Pacific Ocean and San Diego Bay. More retired Navy officers live here than any other place in the US, and although the military presence is high, it's unobtrusive. For over 100 years, visitors have flocked to Coronado to be part of this charmed life. Even with its thriving resorts, restaurants, sidewalk cafés, and unique shops, the village never seems overwhelmed.

Hotel del Coronado
This 1887–8 Queen Anne wooden masterpiece **(right)** is a National Historic Landmark. It was the first hotel west of the Mississippi with electric lights.

NEED TO KNOW
MAP C6 ■ www.coronadovisitor center.com

Hotel del Coronado: 1500 Orange Ave; 619 435 6611; www.hoteldel.com

Meade House: 1101 Star Park Cir

Ferry Landing Market Place: 1201 1st St at B Ave; 619 435 8895; open 10am–9pm daily; www.coronadoferry landing.com

Coronado Museum of History and Art: 1100 Orange Ave; 619 435 7242; open 11am–4pm Wed–Fri, 11am–2pm Tue, Sat & Sun; www.coronado history.org

San Diego Ferry: 619 234 4111; adm $5; www.flag shipsd.com

■ Enjoy a drink in the Babcock & Story Bar at Hotel del Coronado.

■ Excellent historical walking tours depart from Glorietta Bay Inn *(1630 Glorietta Blvd; 619 435 5993; Tue, Thu & Sat at 11am; adm).*

2 Meade House
Author L. Frank Baum produced much of his work at this charming house, found on the edge of Star Park. Today, it is a private residence.

3 US Naval Amphibious Base
South of Coronado, along the Silver Strand, this training camp for the Navy SEALS is off-limits to the public.

4 Coronado Bridge
Connecting San Diego to Coronado since 1969, this 2.2-mile (3.5-km) span **(above)** has won architectural awards for its unique design. Struts and braces in a box girder give it a sleek look.

5 Coronado Central Beach
Coronado's main beach claims a golden swath adjacent to the Hotel del Coronado. Families, fishers, surfers, and swimmers all stake spots, while dog-walkers rule the north end.

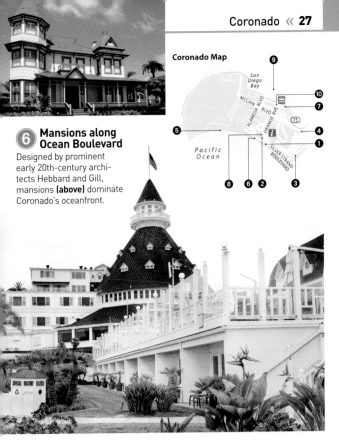

Coronado Map

⑥ Mansions along Ocean Boulevard

Designed by prominent early 20th-century architects Hebbard and Gill, mansions **(above)** dominate Coronado's oceanfront.

⑦ Ferry Landing Marketplace

Next to the ferry dock is a shopping area selling beachwear, jewelry, souvenirs, and art. This is a handy spot to rent a bike or grab a snack.

⑧ Coronado Museum of History and Art

In a 1910 Neo-Classical bank building, galleries exhibit early village history, with photos of the Hotel del Coronado, Tent City, and military memorabilia **(right)**.

⑨ San Diego Ferry

Before the Coronado Bridge, access was only by a long drive around Southern San Diego or via the ferry, which is now only for foot passengers.

⑩ Orange Avenue

The main shopping street has restaurants and sidewalk cafés, as well as a theater and a museum. Independence Day and Christmas parades see residents out celebrating.

L. FRANK BAUM

Beloved American author L. Frank Baum had a strong attachment to Coronado. In 1904, four years after his book *The Wonderful Wizard of Oz* was published, Baum spent the winter at the Hotel del Coronado. He and his wife loved it so much that they returned to the area – and the hotel – almost every winter until 1910. Baum even designed the chandeliers in the hotel's Crown Room. His family later spent time at the Meade House, located close to the hotel.

🔟 ⭐ Point Loma

Point Loma was once one of the roughest areas in San Diego. The city's first boats were tied up here, followed by the largest whaling operation on the West Coast and leather tanning and tallow production. Today, sailboats and lavish yachts grace the marinas of Point Loma, and the waterfront homes make up some of the most expensive real estate in the city. The Cabrillo National Monument offers breathtaking views of the entire city, and is also an excellent place to spy migrating whales from land.

1 Cabrillo National Monument
The spot where, in 1542, Portuguese navigator Cabrillo stepped ashore is on a spit of land at Ballast Point. This statue **(below)** commemorates the first landing of a European expedition on the west coast of the United States.

San Diego skyline, visible from Point Loma

2 Cabrillo National Monument Visitor Center
Browse through books about the Spanish, Native Americans, and early California, or enjoy the daily film screenings. Park rangers are present to answer any questions.

3 Tide Pools
Now protected by law, starfish, anemones, warty sea cucumbers and wooly sculpins thrive in their own little world.

4 Bayside Trail
A 2-mile (3.2-km) round-trip hiking path runs on an old military defense road. Signs on the way identify over 300 indigenous plants such as sage scrub and Indian paintbrush.

5 Sunset Cliffs
A path runs along the edge of these spectacular 400-ft (122-m) high cliffs **(below)**, but signs emphatically warn of their instability. The beach is accessible from Sunset Cliffs Park.

4 miles (6 km) **Point Loma Map**
3 miles (5 km)

Ballast Point

CABRILLO MEMORIAL DRIVE

7 Military Exhibit

After the 1941 Pearl Harbor attack, many felt that San Diego would be the next target. The exhibit explores how the military created a coastal defense system and the largest gun in the US.

8 Whale Overlook

Pacific gray whales migrate yearly to give birth in the warm, sheltered waters of Baja California before heading back to Alaska for a summer of good eating. January and February are the best times to spot whales.

JUAN CABRILLO

After participating in the conquest of Mexico and Guatemala, Juan Cabrillo was instructed to explore the northern limits of the West Coast of New Spain in search of gold and a route to Asia. He arrived at Ballast Point on September 28, 1542, claimed the land for Spain, and named it San Miguel. Cabrillo died a few months later from complications of a broken bone. Spain saw the expedition as a failure and left the territory untouched for more than 200 years.

9 Fort Rosecrans National Cemetery

The southern end of Point Loma belongs to the military installations of Rosecrans Fort. Innumerable crosses mark the graves (above) of more than 100,000 US veterans, some of whom died at the Battle of San Pasqual in the Mexican-American War.

6 Point Loma Nazarene University

Once a yoga commune, much of the original architecture of this Christian university is still intact.

10 Old Point Loma Lighthouse

This Cape Cod-style building was completed in 1855. Unfortunately, coastal fog often hid the beacon light, so another lighthouse, the New Point Loma Lighthouse, was built below the cliff.

NEED TO KNOW

MAP B6

Cabrillo National Monument Visitor Center: 1800 Cabrillo Memorial Dr; 619 523 4285; open 9am–5pm daily; adm $20 per vehicle, $10 per person (cyclists and walk-ins); tickets last for 7 days and

visitors can return as many times as they like; www.nps.gov/cabr

■ Vending machines at the Cabrillo National Monument Visitor Center offer snacks. If you want to spend the day exploring the tide pools or hiking, bring food and water.

■ Bring binoculars to enjoy the views and, if visiting the tide pools, shoes with plenty of grip.

■ The San Diego Metropolitan Transit comes out to the monument. Take bus 28 or 84c from the Old Town Transportation Center.

TOP 10 ★ Mission Basilica San Diego de Alcalá

Founded by Saint Junípero Serra in 1769, this was California's first mission. Harassment by soldiers and lack of supplies caused it to be moved from its original location in Old Town to this site in 1774. The missionaries encouraged the Native Americans to live and work here, and attempted to convert them. In 1775 though, Kumeyaay Native Americans rebelled against the mission, burning it to the ground; it was rebuilt in 1976. After the mission's secularization in 1834, it lay in a state of disrepair, but was restored in 1931.

1 La Casa del Padre Serra

The original 1774 adobe walls and beams **(below)** survived a Native American attack, military occupation, earthquakes, and years of neglect. Padres lived simply, with few material comforts.

2 Campanario

This graceful 46-ft (14-m) bell tower **(right)** defines California mission architecture. One of the bells is considered an original, and the crown atop another suggests it was probably cast in a royal foundry.

3 Padre Luis Jayme Museum

Artifacts here include records of births and deaths in Saint Serra's handwriting, the last crucifix he held, and old photographs showing the extent of the mission's dereliction prior to restoration efforts.

4 Garden Statues

Four charming statues of St. Anthony of Padua **(right)**, patron saint of Christian Native Americans; St. Serra; St. Joseph, saint of Serra's expedition; and St. Francis keep vigil over the inner garden.

5 Chapel

Taken from a Carmelite monastery in Plasencia, Spain, this small chapel features choir stalls, a throne, and an altar dating from the 1300s. The choir stalls are held together by grooves rather than nails. The raised seats allowed the monks to stand while singing.

JUNÍPERO SERRA

Franciscan father Saint Junípero Serra spent 20 years in Mexico before coming to California. Few of his companions survived the tough "Sacred Expedition" across the desert. Serra, undeterred, established California's first mission in 1769. His sainthood was controversial for many Native Americans as they felt the mission system had helped to fragment their culture.

8 Church
The width of a mission church depended on available beams. Restored to specifications of a former 1813 church on this site, it (left) features adobe bricks, the original floor tiles, and wooden door beams.

10 Padre Luis Jayme Memorial
Jayme was killed during the attack on the mission by Kumeyaay warriors in 1775. He was later made California's first martyr; today a cross marks the spot where he died.

Mission Floor Plan

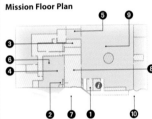

NEED TO KNOW

MAP E3 ■ 10818 San Diego Mission Road ■ www.missionsandiego.org

Open 9am–3:30pm Mon–Fri, 10am–3pm Sat & Sun ■ Adm $3; Tote-a-Tape Tours $2

Church: Mass 7am & 5:30pm Mon–Fri, 5:30pm Sat, 7:30am, 8am, 9am, 10:30am, noon & 5:30pm Sun

■ Food and drinks are not allowed inside the mission.

■ Visitors should note that the San Diego Trolley stops three blocks away.

6 Cemetery
Although it no longer contains real graves, this is the oldest cemetery in California. The crosses are made of original mission tiles. A memorial honors Native Americans who died during the mission era.

7 El Camino Real
Also called the Royal Road or King's Highway, this linked the state's 21 missions, each a day's distance apart on foot.

9 Gardens
Exotic plants add to the lush landscape around the mission (above). With few indigenous Californian species available, missionaries and settlers brought plants from all parts of the world, including cacti from Mexico and bird of paradise from South Africa.

Mission Bay Park

In 1542, seafarer Juan Rodriguez Cabrillo named this tidal basin "False Bay." Between the 1940s and 1960s, the US Army Corps of Engineers transformed the swampland into a 6.5-sq-mile (17-sq-km) showplace aquatic park and the city's premier recreational playground. Containing 19 miles (30 km) of beach and 27 miles (43 km) of shoreline, Mission Bay offers water and land sports, as well as cozy inlets and grassy knolls for lazy days.

4 DeAnza Cove
On the northeast corner of the park, DeAnza is convenient for a picnic or swim. Boats and jet skis launch from the ramp, and there is a designated area for volleyball.

6 Ventura Bridge
Extending 116 ft (35 m) across Mission Bay Drive, Ventura Bridge connects Quivira and Mariners basins, before linking to Mission Beach and Belmont Park.

1 Fiesta Island
Reached via a causeway, this dune-covered peninsular park (above) has bonfire rings and a leash-free dog area. The site also hosts the infamous Over the Line tournament.

2 Mission Bay Aquatic Center
Known as one of the world's largest facilities of its kind, this center at Santa Clara Point offers lessons in nearly every water activity, from surfing and sailing to paddleboard yoga and sea kayaking.

3 Bayside Walk

Strollers, runners, and cyclists may take this route, which follows the beach for almost 5.5 miles (9 km), from Crown Point Park to the park's western edge, where it loops at Mission Point. Rest and take in the views along the path.

5 Mariners Point
Jutting from the tip of a small peninsula, this sandy expanse provides an intriguing dichotomy: it hosts skateboard competitions and is a nesting site for the California least tern (below).

7 Mission Beach and Ocean Front Walk
Parallel to Mission Beach, Ocean Front Walk is more of a movement than a stroll, a chaotic blend of rollerbladers, skate dancers, cyclists, and surfers running toward the waves. Festivities continue onto Mission Beach – a gigantic 2-mile (3-km), year-round beach party.

8 Belmont Park

Belmont Park *(see p59)* still retains its old-fashioned seaside aura, highlighted by the 1925 Giant Dipper roller coaster **(below)**, but there are also attractions like *Tron*-themed laser tag and the FlowBarrel artificial wave machine.

9 Crystal Pier

The dividing line between Pacific and Mission beaches, this 750-ft (228-m) pier **(above)** is notable for its 1930s cottage motel, set right above the water. Even if you don't book a stay at the motel, you can still walk the pier.

Mission Bay Park Map

10 Quivira Basin

Waterfront shops, restaurants, and a resort are clustered around busy Quivira Basin and Dana Landing, from where daily scuba diving and fishing charters depart. Mission Bay Park Headquarters provides information and maps. From Dana Landing, Ingraham Street cuts across Vacation Isle to Crown Point.

NEED TO KNOW

MAP B4 ■ 2581 Quivira Court ■ 619 221 8899 (recorded info 619 221 8824) ■ www.san diego.gov/life guards/about/contact

Mission Bay Aquatic Center: 1001 Santa Clara Place; 858 488 1000; open 9am–7pm daily; equipment available for hire such as sailboats, kayaks, bodyboards, paddleboards, and more (terms and conditions apply); lessons and classes available, rates vary (www.mb aquaticcenter.com).

Belmont Park: 3146 Mission Blvd; 858 488 1549; open 11am–11pm Sun–Thu, 11am–midnight Fri–Sat; ride prices vary (free parking and adm)

■ Several companies offer cruises around Mission Bay. One of the best is Cruise San Diego *(1617 Quivira Rd, www.cruise-sd.com)*, which takes visitors of all ages on stunning sunset cruises around the bay on the Ohana *(7:30pm, days vary; adults $39, children $35)*. It also offers 90-minute Sea Lion tours where you can observe these and other marine animals in their natural habitat *(Sundays 1pm, adults $42, children $25)*. Advance booking is recommended for these popular cruises. The Ohana is docked at the Hyatt Mission Bay.

🔟⭐ La Jolla

Developer Frank Botsford bought a substantial area of barren pueblo land in 1886, which he then subdivided. Other real estate developers soon caught on to La Jolla's potential and built resorts, but it wasn't until Ellen Browning Scripps arrived in 1896 that the town developed as a research, education, and art center. Now, La Jolla (pronounced "hoya") is among the most expensive land in the US. Befittingly, its name translates as "the jewel."

1 La Jolla Bay
This gathering spot **(above)** just below La Jolla village is small but startling, wedged between sandstone cliffs with glorious views. Its robust marine life is protected.

2 La Jolla Playhouse
The Tony Award-winning Playhouse **(below)**, founded by actor Gregory Peck, is housed in the UC San Diego Theatre district *(see p60)*.

3 Museum of Contemporary Art
Only a fraction of more than 3,000 works from every noteworthy art movement since 1950 are on display at this renowned museum.

La Jolla Map

4 Ellen Browning Scripps Park
Stroll along palm-lined walkways and gaze out over panoramic coastline views.

6 Birch Aquarium at Scripps

Brilliantly colored underwater habitats **(left)** educate at this marine museum *(see p59)*. You'll feel like a scuba diver when viewing sharks swimming in an offshore kelp bed housed in a 70,000-gallon tank.

7 Scripps Institution of Oceanography

Leading the way in global science research, Scripps Oceanography is now in its second century of discovery. Hundreds of research programs are under way on every continent and ocean.

8 Torrey Pines State Reserve

At this reserve *(see p52)*, hiking trails wind past coastal scrub, sandstone cliffs, and woodlands, with stunning views of the Pacific. Guided tours are available.

ELLEN BROWNING SCRIPPS

Born in England in 1836, Scripps moved to the US in 1844. She became a teacher, investing her savings in her brother's newspaper ventures in Detroit and Cleveland. Already wealthy, she inherited a fortune on his death in 1900. Scripps spent her last 35 years in La Jolla, giving away millions of dollars for the good of humanity.

9 Salk Institute

Dr. Jonas Salk, creator of the first successful polio vaccine, founded this institution *(see p44)* for biomedical research in 1960.

10 University of California, San Diego (UCSD)

Six colleges make up one of the most prestigious public universities **(below)** in the country.

5 Mount Soledad Veterans Memorial

The 43-ft (13-m) cross on Mount Soledad, erected in 1954, is the centerpiece of a memorial that honors veterans of the Korean and other wars. Six walls beneath the cross hold 2,400 plaques.

NEED TO KNOW

MAP A2

Museum of Contemporary Art: 700 Prospect St; 858 454 3541; open 11am–5pm Thu–Tue; 11am–7pm 3rd Thu each month; adm $10; free 5–7pm third Thu of month; www.mcasd.org

Mount Soledad Veterans Memorial: Soledad Rd; open 7am–10pm daily

Birch Aquarium at Scripps: 2300 Expedition Way; 858 534 3474; open 9am–5pm daily (to 7pm Jul & Aug); adm $19.50 adult, $15 child; www.aquarium.ucsd.edu

Scripps Institution of Oceanography: 8622 Kennel Way; www.sio.ucsd.edu

University of California, San Diego: 9500 Gilman Dr; www.ucsd.edu

■ Stroll the UCSD campus and its Stuart Collection of outdoor sculpture.

TOP 10 ⭐ East County

San Diego's East County offers truly diverse attractions within an hour or so of downtown. Interstate 8 passes casinos and the vintage trains at Campo, with a turnoff to Cuyamaca Rancho State Park. Scenic backroad State Route 78 hits the gold-rush mountain village of Julian. Both roads take in Anza-Borrego Desert State Park.

1 Cuyamaca Rancho State Park

Just 5 miles (8 km) north of I-8, Cuyamaca **(below)** has more than 100 miles (160 km) of hiking, biking, and horse trails, with desert and coast views along the way. A creek meanders through Green Valley.

2 Native American Casinos

Native American communities have more than a dozen 24-hour casinos in the county. Only those over 21 and with valid identification are allowed in gaming areas.

3 Julian

After the gold rush of the 1870s, some stayed on in this charming community **(below)** surrounded by forests in the Cuyamaca Mountains. Filled with B&Bs, this Historical District is a popular weekend getaway and known for its apple orchards.

4 Desert Blooms

On first glimpse, this desert may look like a gigantic expanse of nothingness, but it is rife with life, notably wildflowers **(below)** and bird species. Between February and April, weather permitting, it erupts into a vibrant palette of colorful blooms.

5 Driving Tours

Venturing into the desert by car, other than on the main roads, is not advisable for the inexperienced. Roads can be impassable and unpredictable. A variety of tour operators can safely escort you on everything from a short day tour to an off-road overnight adventure.

⑧ Borrego Springs

San Diego County's desert community **(left)** has lodging, restaurants, tours, and the Park Headquarters, where you can view exhibits, an informative film, and a desert garden.

⑥ Pacific Southwest Railway

Operated by the Railway Museum of San Diego, the *Golden State Limited* departs twice daily on weekends from the historic Campo train depot for a 12-mile (20-km) round trip to Miller Creek.

METAL DINOSAURS

Mexico-born and California resident, sculptor Ricardo Breceda made the metal "dinosaurs" that pop out of the desert-scape. Breceda created more than 130 full-sized replicas of creatures that once roamed these lands, including desert tortoises, saber-toothed cats, wild horses, and a 350-ft (106-m) serpent.

⑨ Anza-Borrego Desert State Park

California's largest state park at 938 sq miles (2,430 sq km), it offers cacti and posies, rough trails, historic roads, mountainous dunes, extreme temperatures, other-worldly skies – plus peace and quiet.

East County Map

⑩ Tecate (Mexico)

Best known for its namesake Tecate beer, this Mexican border town is about 20 minutes west via State Route 94. Check with the Border Patrol for any safety issues, plus re-entry visa. If possible, park your car in the little lot by the border (someone will come out to take a few dollars) and walk across.

⑦ Mount Laguna

After a good winter storm, this 5,738-ft- (1,750-m-) high hamlet at the eastern edge of the Cleveland National Forest becomes a snowy playground for San Diegans, who come here to sled, cross-country ski, and generally marvel at the chillier climes.

NEED TO KNOW
MAP F2

Borrego Springs Chamber of Commerce: 786 Palm Canyon Dr; Borrego Springs; 760 767 5555; www.borregosprings chamber.com

Anza-Borrego Desert State Park Visitor Center: 200 Palm Canyon Dr, Borrego Springs; 760 767 4205; park open dawn–dusk daily, visitor center 9am–5pm Thu–Mon; adm $10 per vehicle; www.parks.ca.gov

■ If crossing the border into Mexico, US citizens and international visitors must have a valid passport for re-entry to the US. Before you go, assure your personal safety and that of your property. Heed US State Department warnings *(www.state.gov/travel)*.

■ The Borrego Springs Chamber of Commerce is a good source for reputable tour operators for off-road excursions and stargazing expeditions.

The Top 10 of Everything

**A stage show at the
La Jolla Playhouse**

Moments in History

① In the Beginning

The Kumeyaay tribe have lived in San Diego since approximately 7,000 BC. Indeed, a skull discovered in 1929 established human presence in this area about 12,000 years ago. The tribe lived in small, organized villages, and subsisted on wild fruits and nuts, game, and fish.

② Arrival of the Spanish

Juan Cabrillo (see p29) was the first European to land at San Diego Bay, making contact with the Kumeyaay tribe. California was regarded as part of the Spanish Empire from this date. In 1602, Sebastian Viscaino celebrated the feast of San Diego de Alcala with the tribe. This event gave the region its name.

Juan Cabrillo

③ The Spanish Settlement (1769)

Fearing the loss of California, Spain sent an expedition, led by Gaspar de Portolá and Franciscan friar Junípero Serra (see p30), to build military posts and Christian missions. This was disastrous for the Native Americans, as the settlers usurped their land.

④ Independence of Mexico (1821)

After gaining independence, Mexico secularized the California missions and gave their land to the politically faithful. The rancho system of land management lasted into the 1900s. Ports were open to all and the city became a center for the hide trade.

In 1850, however, California became part of the US and, later, its 31st state.

⑤ Alonzo Horton's New City (1867)

Real estate developer Alonzo Horton realized an opportunity to develop a city closer to the water than Old Town. He bought 960 acres for $265, and sold or gave it as lots to anyone who could build a brick house. Property values soared, and "New Town" became today's San Diego.

⑥ Transcontinental Railroad (1885)

Interest was renewed in San Diego when the Transcontinental Railroad reached town. Real estate speculators poured in and infrastructure was built. However, Los Angeles seemed more promising, and San Diego's population, having gone from 5,000 to 40,000 in two years, shrank to 16,000.

The Transcontinental Railroad

7 Panama-California Exposition (1915–16)

To celebrate the opening of the Panama Canal and draw economic attention to the first US port of call on the West Coast, Balboa Park (see pp18–19) was made into an attraction. Fair animals found homes at the zoo (see p19) and Spanish-Colonial buildings became park landmarks.

8 California-Pacific Exposition (1935–6)

A new Balboa Park exposition was launched to help alleviate effects of the Great Depression. The architect Richard Requa designed buildings inspired by Aztec, Mayan, and Puebloan themes.

California-Pacific Exposition

9 World War II

The founding of the aircraft industry, spurred by the presence of Ryan Aviation and Convair, gave San Diego an enduring industrial base. After Pearl Harbor, the Pacific Fleet HQ moved here. The harbor was enlarged and hospitals, camps, and housing changed the city's landscape.

10 Later Redevelopment (1981–2022)

Downtown redevelopment brought new life to the area, with the addition of Horton Plaza, the restoration of the historic US Grant Hotel, and the San Diego Convention Center. Today, the city continues to evolve, with the mall at Horton Plaza being demolished in 2020 to make way for The Campus at Horton, a tech hub, scheduled to open in 2022.

TOP 10 FAMOUS SAN DIEGO FIGURES

The author Theodore Geisel

1 Father Luis Jayme (1740–75)
California's first Christian martyr died in a Native American attack (see p31).

2 Richard Henry Dana (1815–82)
Author of the 19th-century classic *Two Years Before the Mast*, a historical record of early San Diego (see p25).

3 Alonzo Horton (1813–1909)
Real estate magnate Horton, the "father" of San Diego, successfully established the city's present location in 1867.

4 Ellen Browning Scripps (1836–1932)
Journalist and philanthropist who funded scientific research at the Scripps Institution of Oceanography (see p35).

5 Wyatt Earp (1848–1929)
Old West sheriff and famed gunman Earp owned saloons and gambling halls in the Gaslamp Quarter (see p12).

6 John D. Spreckels (1853–1926)
Spreckels was the owner of the Hotel del Coronado.

7 L. Frank Baum (1856–1919)
The author of *The Wonderful Wizard of Oz* lived in and considered Coronado an "earthly paradise" (see p26).

8 Kate O. Sessions (1857–1940)
This horticulturalist established the Balboa Park gardens in 1910 (see p21).

9 Theodore Geisel (1904–91)
Best known as the beloved Dr. Seuss, Geisel lived and worked in La Jolla.

10 Dr. Jonas Salk (1914–95)
Developed the first effective polio vaccination and founded the non-profit Salk Institute (see p44) in 1960.

Historic Sites

1 Ballast Point
MAP B6 ■ Point Loma

In 1542, while the Kumeyaay tribe stood on a beach here, Juan Cabrillo *(see p29)* stepped ashore and claimed this piece of land for Spain. In 1803, the "Battle of San Diego Bay" took place at Ballast Point, after Spanish Fort Guijarros fired on an American brig in a smuggling incident.

Entrance to a courtyard in Old Town

2 Old Town

Mexico won its independence from Spain in 1821, after which retired soldiers and their families moved downhill from the presidio, built homes, and opened business-es. An open trade policy attracted others to settle, and by the end of the decade, 600 people lived in Old Town – San Diego's commercial and residential center until 1872.

3 Presidio Hill
MAP P5

Spain established its presence in California atop this hill, and Saint Serra founded the first California mission *(see pp30–31)* here. During the Mexican-American War in 1846, Fort Stockton, made of earthworks on top of the hill, changed hands three times between Mexican and US forces.

4 Lindbergh Field
MAP C5

San Diego International Airport *(see p93)* was popularly called Lindbergh Field after Charles Lindbergh *(see p41)*, who began the first leg of his transatlantic crossing here in 1927. The US Army Air Corps drained the surrounding marshland, took over the small airport, and enlarged the runways to accommodate the heavy bomber aircraft manufactured in San Diego during World War II.

5 Julian
MAP F2

The discovery of gold in the hills northeast of San Diego in 1870 was the largest strike in Southern California. For five years, miners poured into the town of Julian *(see p36)*, which would have become the new county seat if San Diego supporters had not plied the voters of Julian with liquor on election day. The gold eventually ran out, but not until millions of dollars were pumped into San Diego's economy.

6 Mission Basilica San Diego de Alcalá

Originally built on Presidio Hill in 1769, this mission *(see pp30–31)* moved up the valley a few years later. It was the first of 21 missions, as well as the birthplace of Christianity in the state of California. California's first vine-yards were planted here by its founder, Father Junípero Serra. In 1847, the US Cavalry occupied the grounds.

Mission Basilica San Diego de Alcalá

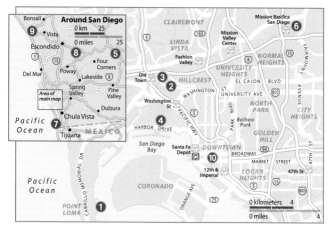

7 Border Field State Park

MAP E3 ■ 619 575 3613

■ Call for opening hours

The Mexican-American War ended with the signing of the Treaty of Guadalupe Hidalgo (see p40) on February 2, 1848. A US and Mexican Boundary Commission then determined the new international border between the two countries, with California divided into Alta and Baja. A marker placed in 1851 on a bluff in this park shows the farthest western point of the new border.

8 San Pasqual Battlefield State Historic Park

MAP E2 ■ 15808 San Pasqual Valley Rd, Escondido ■ Open 10am–4pm Sat & Sun

On December 6, 1846, a volunteer army of Californios, defeated the invading American army in one of the bloodiest battles of the Mexican-American War. Though the Californios won the battle, they later lost the war, and California became part of the USA.

9 Mission San Luis Rey de Francia

Nicknamed the "King of Missions" for its size, wealth, and vast agricultural estates, this mission (see p99) is the largest adobe structure in California. After secularization, it

fell into disrepair and was used for a time as military barracks. The mission has since been restored, and today contains a museum dedicated to the history of the mission era.

10 Gaslamp Quarter

Filled with late-19th-century Victorian architecture, this historic site (see pp12–13) was once the commercial heart of Alonzo Horton's New Town (see p40). When development moved north to Broadway, the area filled with gambling halls and brothels. It was revitalized in the 1970s.

Buildings in the Gaslamp Quarter

🔟 Architectural Highlights

① San Diego County Administration Center

MAP H3 ▪ 1600 Pacific Hwy ▪ Open 8am–5pm Mon–Fri

Four architects responsible for San Diego's look collaborated on this civic landmark. What began as a Spanish-Colonial design evolved into a more "Moderne" 1930s style with intricate Spanish tile work and plaster moldings on the tower.

② Louis Bank of Commerce

Builders of the Hotel del Coronado, the Reid brothers can also take credit for one of the architectural treasures of the Gaslamp Quarter: a stately, four-story twin-towered Victorian structure (see p12). Built in 1888, it was San Diego's first granite building. Of special merit are the ornate bay windows that project from the facade.

③ California Tower and Dome

Bertram Goodhue designed this San Diego landmark (see p19) for the Panama-California Exposition of 1915–16, using Spanish Plateresque, Baroque, and Rococo details. The geometric tile dome imitates Moorish ceramic work often seen in southern Spain. An iron weather vane in the shape of a Spanish ship tops the 200-ft (61-m) tower.

The Mormon Temple lit up at night

④ Mormon Temple

MAP B1 ▪ 7474 Charmant Dr, La Jolla

The temple of the Church of the Latter Day Saints is an ornate, futuristic structure. The golden trumpet-playing angel, Moroni, crowns one of the towers and points the way to Salt Lake City. Interiors are closed to the public.

⑤ Hotel del Coronado

Designed by James and Merritt Reid in 1887, this hotel (see p26) was once the largest in the country to be built entirely of wood. Advanced for its time, the hotel had running bathroom water and telephones, as well as a birdcage elevator.

⑥ Salk Institute

MAP A1 ▪ 10010 N. Torrey Pines Rd ▪ 858 453 4100 ▪ Currently closed due to COVID-19, check website for further details ▪ www.salk.edu

At one of the most famous buildings in San Diego (see p35), twin six-story laboratories comprised of teak panels, concrete and glass stand across from each other, separated by a marble courtyard with a channel of water in the middle. Note architect Louis Kahn's use of "interstitial" space: mechanical devices between floors can change laboratory configurations.

California Tower and Dome

El Cortez
MAP K3 ▪ 702 Ash St

This landmark was once the tallest building and most famous hotel in downtown San Diego. A glass elevator once led to the romantic Sky Room. Ornate Spanish details decorate the reinforced concrete structure, which is now a private condo building.

8 Geisel Library
MAP B1 ▪ UCSD

Named after famed children's author, Dr. Seuss *(see p41)*, and designed by William Pereira, the library at UCSD *(see p35)* has tiers of glass walls supported by reinforced concrete cantilevers. Filmmakers have used it as a backdrop for sci-fi shows.

The Geisel Library at UCSD

9 San Diego Central Library
MAP L4 ▪ 330 Park Blvd ▪ Open 9:30am–5:30pm Mon–Sat

This modern library is a monument to literature and a delightful experience for readers. Step inside to see beautiful open terraces, book-shaped sinks in the lavatories, and a wall made of discarded books in the auditorium.

10 Cabrillo Bridge
MAP K1

Built as an entryway to the 1915–16 Panama-California Exposition, this cantilevered and multiple-arched bridge has a 1,500-ft (457-m) span. The best view of the bridge, especially during Christmas, is from the 163 Freeway below.

TOP 10 PUBLIC ART SIGHTS

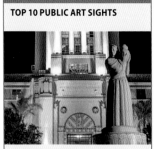

Guardian of Water sculpture

1 Guardian of Water
MAP H3
A 23-ft (70-m) high granite sculpture depicts a pioneer woman.

2 Broadway Fountain in Horton Plaza Park
MAP J5
Ornamental centrepiece with electric lights. Plaques honor city notables.

3 Tunaman's Memorial
MAP B5
A bronze sculpture of three tunamen casting their lines.

4 Magic Carpet Ride
MAP D2
The "Cardiff Kook" surfer statue is often elaborately decorated by pranksters.

5 The Cat in the Hat
MAP B1
The Cat in the Hat looks over Dr. Seuss' shoulder in this bronze sculpture.

6 Surfhenge
MAP E3 ▪ Imperial Beach Pier
Surfboards pay tribute to the surf gods.

7 Woman of Tehuantepec
MAP L2 ▪ House of Hospitality
A 1,200-lb (544-kg) piece of limestone is sculpted into an Aztec woman.

8 Sun God
MAP B1
A fiberglass bird stretches its wings atop a 15-ft (5-m) concrete arch.

9 Paper Vortex
MAP C5 ▪ San Diego International Airport
A paper airplane is artfully transformed into an origami crane.

10 Homecoming
MAP G4 ▪ Navy Pier, Harbor Dr
A bronze sculpture depicts a sailor and his family in a homecoming embrace.

🔟 Museums and Art Galleries

San Diego Museum of Art, Balboa Park

① Museums of Balboa Park

Housed in stunning structures of Spanish-Colonial, Mayan, and Aztec designs, exhibits at these museums *(see pp20–21)* constantly change, making Balboa Park *(see pp18–19)* a year-round attraction. Enjoy fine art, photography, aerospace, anthropology, model trains, and much more.

② Museum of Contemporary Art

The most important contemporary art trends are presented at this museum *(see p79)*. Docent-led tours, lectures, and special family nights make art accessible to all. The museum's flagship facility *(see p34)* is at the former oceanfront home of

Ellen Browning Scripps *(see p35)*, with a satellite location downtown.

③ San Diego Chinese Historical Museum

MAP J5 ■ 404 3rd Ave ■ 619 338 9888 ■ Open 10:30am–4pm Tue–Sat, noon–4pm Sun ■ Adm ■ www.sdchm.org

A wide range of artifacts such as ceramics, bone toothbrushes, and old photographs document a slice of San Diego's history in this Spanish-style building that once served as a Chinese mission. Of note is the ornate bed that once belonged to a Chinese warlord. In the back garden is a koi pond.

④ Tasende Gallery

MAP N2 ■ 820 Prospect St, La Jolla ■ 858 454 3691 ■ www.tasende gallery.com

This gallery presents international contemporary artists. Discover the colorful works of Gaudi-influenced artist Niki de Saint Phalle, the pen-and-ink drawings of Mexico's José Luis Cuevas, and the surrealist paintings of Chilean Roberto Matta, among others.

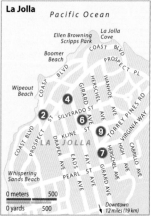

5 Maritime Museum of San Diego

MAP G3 ■ 1492 N. Harbor Dr ■ 619 234 9153 ■ Open 10am–5pm daily ■ Adm ■ www.sdmaritime.org

This fascinating museum pays tribute to the men and ships that so influenced the history and life of San Diego. A range of exhibitions educate and entertain, while several anchored ships can be boarded and explored.

The *Star of India* tall ship, MMSD

6 Sparks Gallery

MAP K5 ■ 530 6th Ave ■ 619 696 1416 ■ www.sparksgallery.com

Housed in the historic Sterling Hardware Building, this is one of San Diego's top galleries. Exhibits span a range of mediums, from photography to sculpture and painting, all by contemporary artists from Southern California.

7 Quint Gallery

MAP N3 ■ 7655 Girard Ave, La Jolla ■ 858 454 3409 ■ www. quintgallery.com

Since 1981, Mark Quint has brought outstanding contemporary artwork to San Diego. Collaborations with collectors, artists, and curators have garnered global acclaim. Exhibited in the 3,000-sq-ft (280-sq-m) space are works by traditional and cutting-edge artists, local and international.

8 Michael J. Wolf Fine Arts

MAP K5 ■ 363 5th Ave ■ 619 702 5388 ■ www.mjwfinearts.com

The oldest gallery in the Gaslamp Quarter features works of emerging US and international contemporary artists. See the urban landscapes of Luigi Rocca, mixed media paintings by Josue Castro, and portraits by Rolling Stone Ronnie Wood.

9 Joseph Bellows Gallery

MAP N3 ■ 7661 Girard Ave, La Jolla ■ 858 456 5620 ■ www.joseph bellows.com

This intimate gallery showcases important vintage prints and contemporary photographs. Three exhibition areas display photography of a superb quality and host a busy program of themed and solo shows. Both renowned and emerging photographers are represented, and past exhibitions have included work by Ansel Adams, Ave Pildas, Dana Montlack, and Wayne Gudmundson.

10 Spanish Village Art Center

In a Spanish village-like atmosphere, adobe houses from the 1935–6 California-Pacific Exposition have been turned into lovely artists' studios, where you can shop or even take a lesson from the artists (see p81).

Spanish Village Art Center

🔟 Beaches

The rugged rocks of Windansea Beach

1 Windansea Beach
MAP N3

Legendary among surfers for its shorebreaks, this beach found literary fame as the setting for Tom Wolfe's *The Pumphouse Gang*. The beach gets a little wider south of the "Shack," a local landmark, but those with small children should still take care.

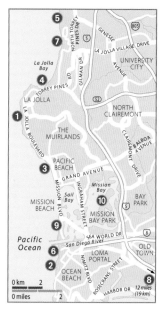

2 Ocean Beach
MAP A4

The laid-back atmosphere of Ocean Beach (see p93) attracts not just locals but also some out-of-towners. Surfers usually go out around the pier, and swimmers farther down the beach. There tends to be a strong rip current at the beach, so it is best not to swim out of sight from a life-guard station. The beach has plenty of facilities, including showers, several picnic tables, and volleyball courts.

3 Pacific Beach

A beach-going spirit fills the air as skateboarders, joggers, and cyclists cruise the promenade parallel to the beach. Chances to people-watch are endless, since Pacific Beach has a reputation for being the place to hang out. Walk out to the Crystal Pier Hotel (see p120), past the bungalows, to watch surfers shooting the curl.

4 La Jolla Shores
MAP Q1

A great family beach with sunbathers, Frisbee-throwers, and boogie-boarders spread out along a broad, sandy white strip lapped by gentle surf, it gets crowded in the summer. Kellogg Park, alongside part of the beach, is a good picnic area for those who forgot their towels. The La Jolla Underwater Ecological Reserve (see p55) is just offshore, so divers are usually out in the water.

5 Torrey Pines State Beach
MAP A1

Miles of sandy beaches and secret coves nestle beneath towering sandstone cliffs. During low tide, tide pools offer a glimpse into life under the sea. Torrey Pines is a San Diego favorite because of its lack of crowds, intimacy, and natural beauty. Parking is available at the Torrey Pines State Reserve *(see p52)* or by the gliderport on top of the cliff.

6 Dog Beach
MAP A4 ■ North end of Ocean Beach at San Diego River

Leashes optional! Your dog can run loose to chase after balls, Frisbees, and other dogs with joyous abandon. The beach is open 24 hours, so you can even come here for a midnight swim. Posts with handy plastic bags help you pick up the aftermath.

Pets playing at Dog Beach

7 Black's Beach
MAP A1

This beach is best known for its nude sunbathers. Access to the beach, which is between Torrey Pines State Beach and La Jolla Shores, is either down an unstable 300-ft (91-m) cliff or via a 1-mile (1.6-km) walk along the beach from either the north or south during low tide. Surfers find the southern end of the beach ideal, as do the hang gliders who launch off from the cliffs above.

8 Coronado Central Beach
MAP C6

Between the iconic Hotel del Coronado and North Island Naval Air Station, along mansion-lined Ocean Avenue, Coronado's municipal beach has been ranked as one of America's best. Its wide swath of golden sand invites sunbathing, sandcastle building, and family fun. Areas are designated for surfers, swimmers, and fishers, and the north end is for dogs and their humans. US Navy SEALS occasionally pop out of the ocean while training.

9 Mission Beach

At this popular beach *(see p101)*, sunburned, sandy bodies vie for space upon the sand, volleyballs and Frisbees fly overhead, and skateboarders and cyclists try to balance drinks and MP3 players as they careen down the boardwalk. If the beach scene gets overwhelming, Belmont Park *(see p59)* is just a block away.

10 Mission Bay Beaches
MAP B4

Protected from the waves of the Pacific Ocean, 27 miles (43 km) of shoreline, including 19 miles (30 km) of sandy beaches, coves, and inlets, offer idyllic picnic locations. On sunny days, the water is filled with sailboats, kayaks, waterskiers, windsurfers, and rowers. Bike paths wind for miles along the shoreline, and wide grassy areas and ocean breezes make flying kites ideal.

Kayakers at a Mission Bay beach

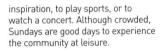

Gardens and Nature Reserves

Hikers at Torrey Pines State Reserve

1 Torrey Pines State Reserve

MAP A1 ■ 12600 N. Torrey Pines Rd ■ 858 755 2063 ■ Open 7:15am–sunset daily ■ Parking fee $10–$25

This stretch of California's wild coast (see p35) offers a glimpse into an ancient ecosystem. Wildflowers bloom along hiking trails that lead past rare Torrey pines and 300 other endangered species. Viewing areas overlook sandstone cliffs to the beach. Spot quail, mule deer, and coyotes.

2 Balboa Park

This landmark destination (see pp18–19) and heart of San Diego offers an array of superb activities. Visit its gardens and museums for

The Lily Pond at Balboa Park

inspiration, to play sports, or to watch a concert. Although crowded, Sundays are good days to experience the community at leisure.

3 Spreckels Park

MAP C6 ■ Coronado

Named after John D. Spreckels (see p41), who donated the land, the park hosts Sunday concerts during the summer as well as art and garden shows. An old-fashioned bandstand, shady trees, green lawns, and picnic tables complete the picture of a small-town community center.

4 Mission Trails Regional Park

MAP F3 ■ 1 Father Junípero Serra Trail

At one of the country's largest urban parks, hiking and biking trails wind along rugged hills and valleys. The San Diego River bisects the park, and a popular trail leads to the Old Mission Dam. The energetic can hike up Cowles Mountain, San Diego's highest peak at 1,591 ft (485 m).

5 Los Peñasquitos Canyon Preserve

MAP E2 ■ 12020 Black Mountain Rd

Archeologists discovered artifacts of the prehistoric La Jolla culture in this ancient canyon. You can also explore the adobe home of San Diego's first Mexican land grant family. Between two large coastal canyons, trails lead past woodland, oak trees, chaparral, and a waterfall.

6 Kate O. Sessions Memorial Park

MAP B3 ■ 5115 Soledad Rd, Pacific Beach

Named in honor of the mother of Balboa Park (see p21), this peaceful spot, with a terrific view of Mission Bay (see p49), is a popular area for picnics. Take advantage of the ocean breezes to rediscover kite flying. Walking trails extend 2 miles (3 km) through a canyon lined with native coastal sage.

7 Mission Bay Park
MAP B4 ■ 2688 E. Mission Bay Dr

This aquatic wonderland (see pp32–3) offers every watersport conceivable. You can also bicycle, play volleyball, jog, or nap on the grass. Excellent park facilities include boat rentals, playgrounds, fire rings, and picnic tables.

8 Ellen Browning Scripps Park
MAP N2

Broad lawns shaded by palms and Monterey cypress trees stretch along the cliffs from La Jolla Cove to Children's Pool (see p58). Promenades offer stunning views of the cliffs and beach.

Ellen Browning Scripps Park

9 Embarcadero Marina Park
MAP H6 ■ Marina Park Way

Join the downtown workers for some fresh air and sunshine. Wide grassy areas and benches give you solitude to enjoy the sweeping views of the harbor. During summer, concerts are held on the lawn.

10 Tijuana River National Estuarine Research Reserve
MAP E3 ■ 301 Caspian Way, Imperial Beach

Serene hiking paths wind through fields of wildflowers and plants. More than 300 species of migratory birds stop by at different times of the year. A visitor center offers information to enhance your experience.

TOP 10 SPECTACULAR VIEWS

Boats at Coronado Bridge

1 Coronado Bridge
MAP C6
Coronado, downtown, and San Diego harbor sparkle both day and night.

2 Point Loma
The breathtaking view from the peninsula's end (see pp28–9) takes in the city, harbor and Pacific Ocean.

3 Mount Soledad
MAP A2
San Diego's most glorious view takes in Coronado, Point Loma, downtown, the valleys, and Mission Bay.

4 Bertrand at Mr. A's
Planes on approach to Lindbergh Field make dining here (see p66) a visual affair.

5 Manchester Grand Hyatt San Diego
The 40th-floor lounge (see p119) offers views of San Diego Bay and Coronado.

6 Torrey Pines State Reserve
The view down the wind-eroded cliffs and across the Pacific is magnificent.

7 Eddie V's Prime Seafood
Every table here (see p67) has water views, but the best spot is the upstairs patio with live jazz.

8 Oceanside's Pier
The historic pier at Oceanside (see p102) provides panoramic views out to sea and along the Pacific Coast Highway.

9 Presidio Park
A panoramic view extends from the freeways in Mission Valley (see p105) below to Mission Bay and the Pacific.

10 Ferries in San Diego Harbor
On a sunny day, nothing beats a ferry ride on the harbor, gazing at the white sailboats against a blue sky.

Previous pages Yachts moored at the San Diego Marina Harbor

Outdoor Activities

① Horseback Riding
Happy Trails: MAP E3; 2606 Hollister St; 619 947 3152; www.ponylandsandiego.com
Guided horseback rides are available on trails, through parks, and on the beach. The South Bay area offers the only beach where you can take an exhilarating ride on the sand and in the waves. There are also pony rides for children.

② Hiking
Hiking is available in every environment imaginable in the San Diego area. Los Peñasquitos Canyon Preserve and Mission Trails Regional Park (see p52) offer trails of varying difficulty through their canyons and valleys; the trails of Torrey Pines State Reserve and Tijuana River National Estuarine Research Reserve (see p53) pass near the ocean. The San Diego Natural History Museum (see p20) hosts guided nature tours.

③ Cycling
Holland's Bikes & Beyond: MAP C6; 1201 1st St, Coronado; 619 435 7180 ▪ iCommute: dial 511 and say "iCommute"; www.icommutesd.com
With over 300 miles (483 km) of bikeways, San Diego is a very cycle-friendly city. iCommute's map details bike rides around the city and county, and is available online.

Sailors enjoying the calm waters

④ Sailing and Boating
Seaforth Boat Rentals: MAP B4; 1641 Quivira Rd, Mission Bay; 888 834 2628; www.seaforthboatrental.com
Whether at Mission Bay or the Pacific Ocean, sailing enthusiasts can rent almost any type of boat, some complete with a crew, champagne, and hors d'oeuvres.

⑤ Surfing
San Diego Surfing Academy: 760 230 1474; www.sandiegosurfing academy.com
San Diego's beaches are famous for surfing. The months with the strongest swells are in late summer and fall, ideally under offshore wind conditions. All the beaches have designated surfing areas.

⑥ Swimming
The Plunge: MAP A4; 3115 Ocean Front Walk; 858 779 1630; www.plungesandiego.com; adm
Nothing beats an ocean dip, though the temperatures seldom exceed 70° F (21° C) even in the summer. Alternatively, most hotels have pools. The Plunge at the Wave House Athletic Club at Mission Beach is great.

Cycling in the sunshine

7 Sportfishing

Seaforth Sportsfishing: MAP B4; 1717 Quivira Rd, Mission Bay; 619 224 3383; www.seaforth landing.com

Albacore, yellowfin, and dorado are just some of the fish in the offshore waters. Summer and fall are the best months, and half-, full-, and multiple-day trips are all available. A fishing license is not required at public piers.

8 Golfing

San Diego CVB: MAP J6; 619 236 1212; www.sandiego.org

With San Diego's perfect climate and amazing views, over 90 public courses and resort hotels offer some of the best golfing in the country. Tee times can be hard to get, so reserve early. The San Diego Convention and Visitors Bureau (CVB) has a golf guide.

A team of golfers at a sand trap

9 Diving

San Diego Ocean Enterprises: MAP B2; 7710 Balboa Ave; 858 565 6054; www.oceanenterprises.com

The best spots for diving off the coast are the giant kelp forests of Point Loma and the La Jolla Underwater Ecological Reserve. Common sealife includes lobsters and garibaldi – the official state marine fish.

10 Skateboarding

Cheap Rentals: MAP A4; 3689 Mission Blvd; 858 488 9070; www.cheap-rentals.com

Mission Bay and Pacific Beach are the best areas to enjoy the miles of pathway shared by rollerbladers and joggers. Some areas prohibit skating, so watch out for the signs.

TOP 10 SPECTATOR SPORTS, TEAMS AND VENUES

1 Rodeos
MAP E2
Catch professional rodeo action at Lakeside, Poway, and Ramona.

2 San Diego Padres
MAP K6 ▪ 100 Park Blvd ▪ 619 795 5000
Petco Park hosts the National League Padres' baseball team.

3 San Diego State University Aztecs
MAP E4
Watch this men's basketball team play at the Qualcomm Stadium.

4 San Diego Gulls Ice Hockey
MAP B4 ▪ Pechanga Arena, 3500 Sports Arena Blvd ▪ 619 224 4625
The San Diego Gulls play in the ECHL Premier AA Hockey League.

5 Del Mar Thoroughbred Club
MAP D2 ▪ 2260 Jimmy Durante Blvd, Del Mar ▪ 858 755 1141
Celebrities and horseracing fans head here to watch the thoroughbreds racing.

6 Hang gliding/Paragliding
Keen hang gliders and paragliders take off from the high ocean cliffs (see p56) located north of La Jolla.

7 San Diego Polo Club
MAP E2 ▪ 3525 Del Mar Heights Rd ▪ 858 876 2248 ▪ www.sandiego polo.com ▪ Adm
Attend polo matches on Sundays.

8 Golf
Watch the annual golf tournaments at Torrey Pines and La Costa.

9 Mission Bay Park
MAP B3
Mission Bay hosts many boating events.

10 San Diego Chargers
MAP D3 ▪ 619 280 2121
Catch this American Football Conference team playing at Qualcomm Stadium.

San Diego Chargers

🔟 Off the Beaten Path

Paragliding at Torrey Pines

1 Paragliding at Torrey Pines

MAP A1 ■ Torrey Pines Gliderport: 2800 Torrey Pines Scenic Dr, La Jolla; 858 452 9858; www.flytorrey.com

Soar off the spectacular cliffs of Torrey Pines (see p52). In your first lesson, you'll receive basic instructions followed by 20–30 minutes of gliding with your instructor. If you'd like to watch for a while before making that exhilarating plunge, a viewing area and café sit on the cliff's edge.

2 Gambling at Native American Casinos

Barona Resort & Casino: MAP E2; 1932 Wildcat Canyon Rd, Lakeside; 619 443 2300 ■ Viejas Casino: MAP E2; 5000 Willows Rd, Alpine; 619 445 5400

Feeling lucky? A dozen casinos promise non-stop Las Vegas-style action and jackpots galore. Starting as a small bingo hall 20 years ago, Native American gaming is now a billion-dollar industry of resort hotels, concert venues, and golf courses. Today, San Diego County has the highest concentration of casinos in the state of California. Thousands of slot machines, video poker, and gaming tables in immense, striking buildings will satisfy the gambler in you.

3 Rent a Harley Davidson

MAP H2 ■ Eagle Rider of San Diego: 4645 Morena Blvd; 619 369 9480; www.eaglerider.com

Born to be wild? Don your jeans and a black leather jacket and rent a bike for a day. You won't be alone: droves of bikers take to the highway, especially on weekends. The back-country of San Diego County is a prime area for powering a Fat Boy, Road King, or Dyna Wide Glide down the road.

4 Biplane Flying

MAP D3 ■ San Diego Air Tours: Montgomery Field; 800 359 2939 ■ www.airtoursofsandiego.com

Two of you sit in the front cockpit of a restored 1920s biplane wearing helmet and goggles, and soar over beaches, lakes, golf courses, and houses, while the pilot flies behind. The *Beech Belle*, a World War II VIP biplane, is great for that special occasion. For an extra thrill, ask the pilot to put you through aerobatic loops and rolls.

5 Pick Your Own Strawberries

MAP D2 ■ Carlsbad Strawberry Company: 1050 Cannon Rd, Carlsbad; 760 603 9608; www. carlsbadstrawberry company.com

For a fun family experience with a family-run business, pick your own fresh, tasty California

Carlsbad Strawberry Company

strawberries straight from the vine. Strawberry season runs from late January to mid-July, weather permitting. There is plenty to do in the autumn too, including visiting the Pumpkin Patch, taking a tractor ride, or following the trail through the Corn Maze.

6 Tall Ship Adventure Sail

Take a three-hour adventure aboard *The Californian*, the State of California's official tall ship and a replica of a Gold Rush-era cutter. Passengers can assist in manning the helm, hauling the line, and the end-of-day cannon salute. Crew members tell whaling and battle tales and of San Diego's sailing past. Booking is advised; departure is from the Maritime Museum *(see p47)*.

7 UFO Spotting in East County
MAP F1

Several San Diego groups take UFO (Unidentified Flying Object) sightings seriously. The best places to spot UFOs are in Borrego Springs and Ocotillo Wells. Given San Diego's strong military presence, that saucer in the sky might well be a secret government mission.

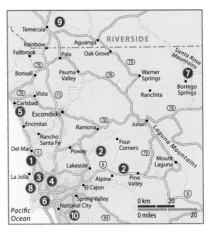

Hot-air balloon

8 Diving at Wreck Alley
MAP A4

Just off Mission Beach is the final resting place for the *Yukon*, a decommissioned Canadian warship, the coastguard cutter *Ruby E*, and a barge, all deliberately sunk to create an artificial reef. A research tower here collapsed on its own, with its dangling wires and protrusions only adding to the otherworldly, ethereal

atmosphere. Thousands of invertebrate marine creatures live here. Charter boats will take you out.

9 Hot-Air Ballooning
MAP E1 ■ California Dreamin': 33133 Vista del Monte Rd, Temecula; 951 699 0601; www.california dreamin.com

You can watch or take part in inflating a brilliantly colored balloon. Hop in the basket and begin to float over the valleys and hills with a glass of champagne in hand. Balloon rides take flight above the Temecula wine country at sunrise and the Del Mar coastline at sunset.

10 Steam Train Rides
MAP D3 ■ Chula Vista Live Steamers: Rohr Park, 4548 Sweetwater Rd, Bonita; 760 815 0978; www. chulavistalivesteamers.org

Run by ordinary people who happen to love all things steam – lawn mowers, tractors, cranes, boats, and trains, Chula Vista is dedicated to maintaining the tracks of the Sweetwater & Rohr Park Railroad. The members offer free rides (donations appreciated) on the steam locomotive during the second weekend of each month.

Children's Attractions

A horse at the Balboa Park Carousel

① Balboa Park Carousel
MAP L2 ■ Balboa Park ■ Adm

Kids will love the carved animals and hand-painted murals of this unique 1910 carousel, right by the zoo. Its Brass Ring game gives riders the chance to win a free turn.

② San Diego Zoo
During seasonal holidays and summer, Dr. Zoolittle presents his entertaining science shows and guest performers delight the crowds. The zoo *(see p19)* also offers summer camps and art classes, while special family events are held throughout the year.

③ LEGOLAND®
Children are fascinated by the 30 million plastic bricks fashioned into famous landmarks and life-sized African animals. In Fun Town, kids can drive electric cars or pilot a helicopter; at the Imagination Zone, they can build robots. Other attractions here *(see p102)* include a 4D movie adventure and a waterpark.

④ Adventure Kids in Egypt at the San Diego Museum of Us
On the museum's *(see p20)* second floor, kids dress up as pharaohs and learn about ancient Egypt by building a pyramid, deciphering hieroglyphics, and listening to the god Anubis explain the mummification process. At a re-creation of an archeological dig, kids dig through sand for treasure and also learn to identify an artifact's age.

⑤ Marie Hitchcock Puppet Theater in Balboa Park
MAP L2 ■ Balboa Park ■ 619 544 9203 ■ Adm ■ www.balboapark puppets.com

Named after the park's beloved and skilled "puppet lady," the Balboa Park Puppet Guild houses a wonderful collection of marionettes and hand, rod, and shadow puppets. The Magic of Ventriloquism, Pinocchio, and Grimm's classics are some of the shows here.

⑥ Harbor Seal-Watching at Children's Pool
MAP N2 ■ Coast Blvd & Jenner St, La Jolla

Children used to swim at this sheltered cove, but harbor seals had much the same idea. The seals are protected by federal law so the beach is now closed, and children must view the entertaining crowds of wild marine animals swimming and sleeping from behind a rope.

⑦ Reuben H. Fleet Science Center
MAP M1 ■ 1875 El Prado ■ 619 238 1233 ■ Open 10am–5pm daily (to 6pm Fri–Sun) ■ Adm ■ www.fleetscience.org

Science can be fun for all. At Kid City, children aged 2–5 can play with conveyor belts, air chutes, and colorful foam blocks. Older kids go wild building complex structures at Block Busters! and enjoy other hands-on areas. In the Virtual Zone, kids can explore symmetry in time as a video camera records movement.

8 San Diego Zoo Safari Park

This park *(see p99)* has more than 3,000 wild and endangered animals from Africa, Europe, Asia, North and South America, and Australia. Herds of animals roam freely in enclosures that replicate their natural habitats. Compatible animals are mixed, allowing visitors to observe their interactions. Kids can enjoy the safari adventures – ziplines, cheetah runs, and an open-air caravan are among the most popular attractions.

9 Belmont Park

MAP A4 ■ **3146 Mission Blvd**
■ **858 488 1549** ■ **Adm for rides**

This old-fashioned fun zone keeps the kids entertained for hours. They can board the Giant Dipper roller coaster, take a ride on the Tilt-a-Whirl, and go on an antique carousel; enjoy the Bumper Cars; or climb high above the ground on the challenging Sky Ropes Adventure. For indoor adventures, there's Laser Tag, Laser Maze, rock climbing, and mini golf.

10 Birch Aquarium at Scripps

MAP Q1 ■ **2300 Expedition Way**
■ **858 534 3474** ■ **Open 9am–5pm daily** ■ **Adm** ■ **www.aquarium. ucsd.edu**

Coral reefs, seahorses, octopi, and undulating jellyfish have a high ooh-and-ah factor for kids. The aquarium presents special educational activities, scavenger hunts, and craft workshops throughout the year, among more than 30 tanks filled with brilliantly colored fish. Kids love the sea-dragon display and the baby seahorse nursery.

The Giant Dipper at Belmont Park

Performing Arts Venues

① The Old Globe
MAP L1 ▪ 1363 Old Globe Way ▪ 619 234 5623 ▪ Check event schedule ▪ www.theoldglobe.org
Every year 250,000 people attend performances at the three theaters in this complex: the 600-seat Old Globe Theatre, the intimate White Theatre, and the outdoor Davies Theatre, which hosts a Shakespeare festival in the summer.

The Old Globe, built in 1935

② La Jolla Playhouse
MAP B1 ▪ La Jolla Village Dr at Torrey Pines Rd, UCSD Campus, La Jolla ▪ 858 550 1010
Gregory Peck, Mel Ferrer, and Dorothy McGuire founded this theater in 1947. All the Hollywood greats once performed here. Now affiliated with UCSD, the theater has been the debut stage for several plays that have gone on to win the Tony award.

③ San Diego Civic Theatre
MAP J4 ▪ 1100 3rd Ave ▪ 619 570 1100
If you missed the latest Broadway show, don't worry: chances are the touring company will perform at this grand theater. Featuring local talent and the world's most acclaimed stars, the San Diego Opera stages four annual productions here.

④ Lyceum Theatre
MAP J4 ▪ 79 Horton Plaza ▪ 619 544 1000
Two theaters are part of the San Diego Repertory Theatre complex: the 550-seat Lyceum and the 270-seat Lyceum Space Theatre. Shows run from the experimental to multilingual performances and Shakespeare with a modern slant. In addition, the theater hosts visiting companies and art exhibitions.

⑤ Balboa Theatre
MAP J4 ▪ 868 Fourth Ave ▪ 619 564 3000 ▪ www.broadway sd.com
With Moorish and Spanish Revival decor, this beautifully renovated downtown theater (see p13) inside a historic vaudeville palace stages touring Broadway shows. It is also home to the city's annual Mainly Mozart Festival (see p73).

⑥ Humphrey's Concerts by the Bay
MAP B5 ▪ 2241 Shelter Island Dr, Shelter Island ▪ 619 224 3577
From May to October, jazz, rock, comedy, blues, folk, and world music are performed in an outdoor 1,350-seat amphitheater next to San Diego Bay. Special packages to Humphrey's Restaurant and Humphrey's Half Moon Inn (see p119) are available to patrons.

Humphrey's Concerts by the Bay

7 Theatre in Old Town

MAP P5 ■ 4040 Twiggs St
■ 619 337 1525

Only 250 amphitheater-style seats wrap around the stage of this theater in an Old Town barn. Leading local company Cygnet Theatre performs dramas, musicals, and comedies such as *The History Boys*, *A Little Night Music*, and *A Christmas Carol*.

8 Spreckels Theatre

MAP J4 ■ 121 Broadway
■ 619 235 9500

Commissioned by John D. Spreckels *(see p41)*, this Neo-Baroque land-mark has murals, classical statuary, and an elegant marble lobby. It is currently being renovated and will re-open as a concert venue.

Ornate interior, Spreckels Theatre

9 North Island Credit Union Amphitheatre

MAP E3 ■ 2050 Entertainment Cir, Chula Vista ■ 619 494 5600

Major pop artists perform from March to October in this notable open-air amphitheater. Great sight lines and giant video screens ensure a good view. There is seating for 10,000 people and the grass can accommodate another 10,000.

10 Copley Symphony Hall

MAP K4 ■ 750 B St ■ 619 235 0804

Formerly known as Fox Theatre, a Rococo-Spanish Renaissance extrava-ganza built in 1929, this venue was to be destroyed until developers donated it to the San Diego Symphony in 1984. Since restored, the hall hosts excel-lent classical music concerts.

TOP 10 MOVIES FILMED IN SAN DIEGO

Sands of Iwo Jima, 1949

1 Citizen Kane, 1941
Director and actor Orson Welles used the California Tower and Dome *(see p19)* in Balboa Park as Xanadu.

2 Sands of Iwo Jima, 1949
John Wayne raced up a hill at Camp Pendleton, the setting for the World War II battle in the acclaimed film.

3 Some Like It Hot, 1959
Hotel del Coronado *(see p26)* formed a backdrop for Marilyn Monroe, Jack Lemmon, and Tony Curtis in this film.

4 MacArthur, 1971
Gregory Peck, born in La Jolla in San Diego, played the eponymous general on Silver Strand State Beach.

5 Attack of the Killer Tomatoes, 1978
Filmed entirely in San Diego, this film's settings include the UCSD campus and the majestic *Star of India* sailing ship.

6 The Stunt Man, 1980
This film had several stuntmen jumping off the roof of Hotel del Coronado.

7 Top Gun, 1986
Tom Cruise chatted up Kelly McGillis at the iconic Kansas City Barbecue, in the harbor district.

8 Almost Famous, 1999
Nothing much had to be changed for the Volkswagen and Birkenstock look of 1970s Ocean Beach *(see p48)*.

9 Pearl Harbor, 2000
Kate Beckinsale proved her love for Ben Affleck by bidding him goodbye at the San Diego Railroad Museum in Campo.

10 Traffic, 2000
Along with scenes of San Diego and Tijuana, *Traffic's* car explosion took place in the judges' parking lot of the Hall of Justice.

Nightlife

Plush interior of Prohibition

1 Prohibition
MAP K5 ▪ 548 5th Ave ▪ Closed Sun & Mon ▪ Adm ▪ Dress code on Fri & Sat ▪ www.prohibitionsd.com

A small, intimate jazz bar with perfect martinis and a laid-back crowd that comes for the great music and exceptional service. The bar has the feel of a private members club but it welcomes all.

2 Onyx Room
MAP K5 ▪ 852 5th Ave ▪ 619 876 8044 ▪ Open Fri & Sat ▪ Adm ▪ www.onyxroom.com

At this chic basement club, order the cocktail of the month and settle back in a vibrant lounge atmosphere. Upstairs is the Onyx's sister bar Thin, where the unique "engineered" drinks are served in an urbane atmosphere.

3 Fluxx
MAP J5 ▪ 500 4th Ave ▪ 619 467 6653 ▪ Open 9pm–2am Thu–Sat ▪ Adm ▪ Dress code applies ▪ www.fluxxsd.com

More of an experience than a club, Fluxx showcases top music events, custom sound and lighting, a huge dance floor, a VIP section, and bottle service. DJs mix up hip-hop, top 40, rock, and electronic sounds.

4 El Dorado Cocktail Lounge
MAP K4 ▪ 1030 Broadway ▪ 619 237 0550 ▪ Adm ▪ www.eldoradobar.com

This classy boutique martini lounge with Wild West bordello-themed decor offers an amazing variety of entertainment, such as dance parties, DJs, live music, and art shows. The nightly events, top-notch service, and exceptional variety of drinks draw in the crowds.

5 The Rooftop by STK
MAP K5 ▪ 600 F St ▪ 619 814 2002 ▪ Open 4–9pm Mon–Thu, 2–9pm Fri–Sat ▪ Adm

Located inside the Andaz Hotel, this glittering nightspot is filled with dancers all week. An open-air rooftop lounge combines DJ sets with private cabanas and panoramic views of the downtown skyline.

6 Cafe Sevilla
MAP K5 ▪ 353 5th Ave ▪ 619 233 5979 ▪ Adm ▪ www.cafesevilla.com

This restaurant-nightclub offers dancing. Tango and flamenco dinner shows are held in the Spanish restaurant, while instructors teach salsa and samba downstairs. You can practice your moves to the live bands that perform salsa, flamenco, and rumba music afterward. The basement also becomes a dance club every night.

Latin-style decor at Cafe Sevilla

7 Casbah

MAP H2 ▪ 2501 Kettner Blvd ▪ 619 232 4355 ▪ Adm ▪ www.casbah music.com

Underground alternative rock rules at this club. Famous and future bands turn up the decibels every night. Past headliners have included The Dillinger Escape Plan and The Kills.

8 The Tipsy Crow

MAP K5 ▪ 770 5th Ave ▪ 619 338 9300 ▪ Adm after 9:30pm Thu & after 8:30pm Fri & Sat ▪ www.thetipsy crow.com

The Tipsy Crow occupies three floors. Upstairs are marble fireplaces, tapestries, and a library; on the ground level, a mahogany bar serves drinks; while the downstairs hosts live music and the Gaslamp Comedy Show.

Exterior of The Tipsy Crow

9 Humphrey's Backstage Live

MAP B5 ▪ 2241 Shelter Island Dr ▪ 619 224 3577 ▪ Adm for most bands ▪ www.humphreysbackstagelive.com

Enjoy a variety of live music nightly at this waterfront lounge with an unbeatable view of the bay. Come early for a terrific happy hour.

10 National Comedy Theatre

MAP C4 ▪ 3717 India St ▪ 619 295 4999 ▪ Adm ▪ www.nationalcomedy.com

Held on Fridays and Saturdays, the National Comedy Theatre's improvisational shows are family-friendly and popular. The audience chooses a game for each show, and decides the winner.

TOP 10 LGBTQ+ VENUES

The main dance floor at Spin

1 Spin
MAP C4 ▪ 2028 Hancock St ▪ 619 294 9590
Three floors of bars and a dance club.

2 Cheers of San Diego
MAP D4 ▪ 1839 Adams Ave ▪ 619 298 3269
This dependably divey beer and wine bar has been in business since 1982.

3 The Rail
MAP C4 ▪ 3796 5th Ave ▪ 619 298 2233
San Diego's oldest LGBTQ+ bar.

4 Urban Mo's Bar & Grill
MAP C4 ▪ 308 University Ave ▪ 619 491 0400
Rowdy drag club open to all.

5 Pecs
MAP C4 ▪ 2046 University Ave ▪ 619 296 0889
Gay Harley-Davidson enthusiasts frequent this popular bar.

6 The Gossip Grill
MAP C4 ▪ 1220 University Ave ▪ 619 260 8023
LGBTQ+ restaurant and bar that transforms into a dance club nightly.

7 Number One Fifth Ave
MAP C4 ▪ 3845 5th Ave ▪ 619 299 1911
Video bar, pool table, and patio.

8 Flicks
MAP D4 ▪ 1017 University Ave ▪ 619 297 2056
Cocktails, dancing, and sing-alongs.

9 Rich's
MAP C4 ▪ 1051 University Ave ▪ 619 578 9349
Go-go dancers perform here.

10 Lips San Diego
MAP D4 ▪ 3036 El Cajon Blvd ▪ 619 295 7900
Drag shows and crowded Sunday brunches, with a cover charge.

Cafés and Bars

1 Cafe-Bar Europa – The Turquoise
MAP A3 ■ 873 Turquoise St ■ 858 488 4200

Reminiscent of the bars of Bohemian Europe, this Pacific Beach café exudes tradition in a high-speed world. You can even philosophize over a glass of absinthe. Tapas are the featured fare in the restaurant, and live entertainment is scheduled most nights.

2 La Sala
MAP N2 ■ La Valencia Hotel, La Jolla

Sitting in the hotel's (see p118) lobby lounge amid Spanish mosaics, hand-painted ceilings and murals, red-tiled floors, and huge palms is like being in a Spanish palace. Order a drink and gaze out at the ocean; a pianist plays in the evening. On sunny days, take advantage of the outside tables.

3 Habano's Café & Cigar Lounge
MAP B4 ■ 4004 Sports Arena Blvd ■ 619 269 4308

Buy a cigar from the huge stock in the walk-in humidor, then light up in a rustic setting with big, comfortable furniture or on the patio. There are also craft beers, espresso, tapas, and panini. Bands play on weekends.

Lestat's Coffee House

4 Bean Bar
MAP K6 ■ 1068 K St ■ 619 269 2887

Baristas make your coffee from the finest beans at this East Village neighborhood café, small in size but big on quality. Service is friendly, beverages are diligently prepared, and the proprietors firmly believe in fair trade.

5 Lestat's Coffee House
MAP D4 ■ 3343 Adams Ave ■ 619 272 3259

Named after the character in Anne Rice's vampire novels, this café in a hip spot serves coffee and pastries 24 hours a day. Local bands entertain in the evening. There's free Wi-Fi, too.

6 The Field Irish Pub
MAP K5 ■ 544 5th Ave ■ 619 232 9840

Literally imported from Ireland, the wood walls, flooring, decorations, and assorted curios were shipped over and reassembled. The bartenders and waitstaff extend true Irish hospitality; not to mention the Guinness. Grab a sidewalk seat on Fifth Avenue or try for a window seat upstairs. The pub food is also great.

St. Patrick's Day at The Field Irish Pub

7 Twiggs Bakery & Coffee House

MAP D4 ▪ 4590 Park Blvd
▪ 619 296 0616

Enjoy a latte and a snack in this fun café. It's packed all day with locals. On the second and fourth Mondays of each month, you'll find poetry readings being held here.

8 Top of the Hyatt

Window seats at this bar in the Manchester Grand Hyatt hotel (see p119) are at a premium at sunset, offering breathtaking views of the bay, Coronado, Point Loma, and the jets over Lindbergh Field. Dark woods exude a sedate, plush atmosphere, with drink prices to match.

Elegant interior of the Top of the Hyatt

9 Wet Stone Wine Bar & Café

MAP J4 ▪ 1927 4th Ave
▪ 619 255 2856

Chef/owner Christian Gomez serves bold dishes in an intimate, eclectic space with tropical plants, against a soundtrack of sultry rhythms. Carefully selected wines are available by the glass or bottle.

10 Waterfront Bar & Grill

MAP H3 ▪ 2044 Kettner Blvd
▪ 619 232 9656

San Diego's oldest tavern opened shortly after Prohibition ended. Customers at this basic watering hole ranged from laborers to lawyers, and the present clientele is still diverse. Business is brisk, the bar is fully stocked, and burgers and light fare are on the menu.

TOP 10 BREAKFAST SPOTS

Outdoor seating at The Cottage

1 The Cottage
Enjoy the freshly-baked cinnamon rolls and Belgian waffles here (see p101).

2 Café 222
MAP J5 ▪ 222 Island Ave ▪ 619 236 9902 ▪ $
Try Café 222's pumpkin waffles and French toast.

3 Brockton Villa
Start the morning here (see p104) with crêpes, omelets, or a "tower of bagel."

4 Crown Room
MAP C6 ▪ Hotel del Coronado
The room (see p26) is legendary, and the Sunday feast amazing.

5 Hash House A Go Go
MAP C4 ▪ 3628 5th Ave ▪ 619 298 4646 ▪ $
Locals vote this hip, award-winning café the best breakfast spot in town.

6 Hob Nob Hill
MAP J2 ▪ 2271 1st Ave ▪ 619 239 8176 ▪ $
Enjoy waffles, omelets, and pancakes.

7 Broken Yoke Café
MAP A3 ▪ 1851 Garnet Ave ▪ 858 270 9655 ▪ $
Choose from 30 varieties of omelets.

8 Kono's Café
MAP A3 ▪ 704 Garnet Ave ▪ 858 483 1669 ▪ No credit cards ▪ $
Join the line for banana pancakes and breakfast burritos.

9 Richard Walker's Pancake House
MAP J5 ▪ 520 Front St
▪ 619 231 7777 ▪ $
More than 100 items are offered here.

10 The Mission
MAP A3 ▪ 3795 Mission Blvd
▪ 858 488 9060 ▪ $
Breakfast is served until 3pm in this funky café.

For a key to price ranges see p83

📖10 Restaurants

A dining room with a view at Bertrand at Mr. A's

1 Bertrand at Mr. A's

For casually elegant dining with a dazzling view, this restaurant *(see p89)* with friendly staff is hard to beat. Inspired by contemporary French-Mediterranean cuisine, the seasonal menu of American dishes is the star here. Unusual for San Diego, there is a dress code here that asks diners to leave shorts and casual wear at home.

2 Island Prime

Presided over by chef Deborah Scott, the scrumptious New American cuisine at Island Prime *(see p97)* includes fresh seafood, prime steaks, mouthwatering "Deborah's Compositions," as well as fine wines. The C Level bar (with a happy hour) offers appetizers and more filling fare.

3 El Agave Tequileria

Ancient Mexican and Spanish spices and traditions make for a unique Mexican dining experience *(see p89)*. Shrimp, sea bass, and the filet mignon prepared with goat's cheese and a dark tequila sauce are heavenly. Mole, the distinctive blending of spices, garlic, and sometimes even chocolate, is a specialty. There are some 150 tequila selections here as well.

4 The Marine Room

Guests can dine on exciting, romantic global cuisine derived from French classics at this restaurant *(see p105)*. If you're not that hungry and would like to enjoy the sunset, opt for the hors d'oeuvres in the lounge.

5 Sushi Ota

Don't be fooled by the modest exterior: this is possibly San Diego's most cherished restaurant *(see p105)* for an authentic Japanese experience and all things sushi, as proven by the many Japanese patrons. The restaurant is also famous for its sea urchin dishes.

6 Baci Ristorante

Classic Italian cuisine is presented in this subtly modern restaurant *(see p105)* with Old World charm. The menu includes creative specials, as well as traditional dishes. The tuxedo-clad waiters, who have been there for years, deliver excellent service.

7 The Prado at Balboa Park

Hand-painted ceilings, glass sculptures, and whimsical artwork adorn this atmospheric restaurant *(see p83)*. A large terrace overlooks the gardens of Balboa Park. A variety of margaritas and drinks from around South America complement an excellent cuisine best described as Latin and Italian fusion.

8 Filippi's Pizza Grotto

At this Little Italy favorite *(see p83)*, the red-checkered table-cloths, dim lights, and hundreds of Chianti bottles hanging from the ceiling haven't changed in decades. Enter through the Italian deli in front to get to the authentic dishes on offer.

9 Eddie V's Prime Seafood

Views of La Jolla Cove loom from every table of this casually upscale restaurant *(see p105)*. Mouth-melting seafood, selections from the oyster bar, and comfort-food sides pair with wines from the highly praised cellar. Live jazz plays nightly on the upper level patio.

Tuna dish at Eddie V's Prime Seafood

10 Emerald Chinese Seafood Restaurant

San Diego's best Chinese restaurants are found in Kearny Mesa. Locals pack into this large dining room *(see p105)* to enjoy lunchtime dim sum and fresh, simple but exquisitely prepared seafood dishes at dinner.

TOP 10 ROMANTIC RESTAURANTS

The waterfront Island Prime

1 Island Prime
Stunning views of Coronado and the city skyline complement the superb cuisine on offer here *(see p97)*.

2 Seréa
Exquisite seafood and impeccable service at this impressive spot *(see p97)*.

3 Mille Fleurs
A charming French restaurant *(see p105)* with top service and a great wine list.

4 Chez Loma
Delicious French cuisine here *(see p97)* creates the ingredients for romance.

5 Old Venice
MAP B5 ▪ 2910 Cañon St ▪ 619 222 5888 ▪ $$
A casually elegant venue that's not too pricey in Point Loma.

6 Addison
MAP D2 ▪ 5200 Grand Del Mar Way ▪ 858 314 1900 ▪ $$$
Old-world elegance sets the scene for modern French cuisine at San Diego's first Michelin-starred restaurant.

7 The WineSellar & Brasserie
MAP D2 ▪ 9550 Waples St, Suite 115 ▪ 858 450 9557 ▪ $$$
A delightful brasserie with excellent wine tasting.

8 The Marine Room
Haute cuisine, candlelight, and soft music *(see p66)*.

9 George's at the Cove
MAP P2 ▪ 1250 Prospect St ▪ 858 454 4244 ▪ $$$
The most popular place to propose in San Diego.

10 Il Fornaio
An intimate fine dining restaurant with waterfront views and delicious Italian specialties *(see p97)*.

For a key to restaurant price ranges see p83

🔟 Stores and Shopping Centers

1 Liberty Station

Formerly the Naval Training Center, this waterfront compendium *(see p96)* of Spanish Colonial-Revival buildings now welcomes shoppers with its many grocery stores, art galleries, and wine bars. Monthly art walks and live entertainment are free, as is parking.

2 Fashion Valley

This ritzy shopping center *(see p88)* contains six major department stores, including Neiman Marcus and Bloomingdale's, as well as 200 specialty boutiques. Tiffany & Co., MAC cosmetics, and Louis Vuitton are just a few of the stores found here. The most famous store, however, is the luxury department chain Nordstrom, which holds an almost cult-like status among shopping fanatics. "Nordies" remains as popular as ever for its vast clothing selection and impressive shoe

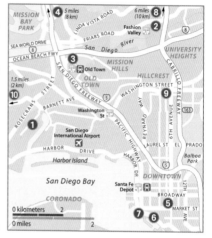

Fashion Valley shopping center

department. The San Diego Trolley conveniently stops in the parking lot.

3 Bazaar del Mundo
MAP N5

Run by Diane Powers, a successful entrepreneur and design expert, this colorful market in the Old Town is made up of a collection of independent shops. Expect unique, carefully curated, and handmade items from Latin America and around the world, including women's clothes, jewelry, folk art pieces, home decor, and Fair Trade items.

4 Pangea Outpost
MAP A3

Found just north of Mission Bay, this super-cool spot is housed in a red-brick building with an eye-catching mural on the outside. Inside are over 70 small businesses selling an eclectic range of items made by local and international artisans and artists. Head here to pick up things like handmade jewelry, quirky artwork, and locally made candles, among much more.

5 The Wine Bank

A regular clientele of wine connoisseurs frequent this intimate Gaslamp Quarter business (see p81). Hundreds of offerings from California and the rest of the world are found on two floors. The expertise of its wine professionals will help in your selection of fine wines in all price ranges. Call for the latest wine tasting schedule.

6 Girard Avenue & Prospect Street

MAP N2

These intersecting streets in La Jolla are synonymous with upscale shopping and high-end art galleries. If you're seeking an expensive look, chic clothing boutiques and Italian shoe stores will happily oblige. The gorgeous displays in the home decor shops will give you great ideas to take home. In the breezy arcades, don't miss the one-of-a-kind shops and beachwear boutiques.

7 Seaport Village

If you're looking for souvenirs or that unusual knick-knack for the shelf, this is the right place (see p81). The Village's superb location along San Diego's waterfront will keep you occupied. Each summer, the Busker Fest brings street performers here from across the country to entertain.

8 REI

To participate in San Diego's outdoor life, you might need sports equipment. This store (see p103) has it all, including rentals of camping gear, snowshoes, and tents, as well as a full-service bike shop. You can also take bike lessons, enjoy lectures, and sign up for photography classes.

Secondhand store on Fifth Avenue

9 University and Fifth Avenues

MAP C4

In Uptown, near the intersection of University and Fifth Avenues, the predominately LGBTQ+ Hillcrest neighborhood (see p88) is a haven of fun and enticing shops, cafés, restaurants, and bars. Bookshops, resale wear, and vinyl record stores are among the independent businesses.

10 Newport Avenue

MAP A4

This is not just the main road through town; it is also one big blast into the past before the street hits the beach. You can pick up anything from Arts and Crafts-era pottery to tie-dye T-shirts. Street parking is available.

The waterfront Seaport Village

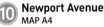

San Diego for Free

Seals lying around the Children's Pool in La Jolla

① Whales, Dolphins, and Seals

In season, you can often see migrating whales while staring out to sea. The same is true for dolphins, especially in the Encinitas area. Harbor seals can be seen lazing around the Children's Pool in La Jolla (see p58).

② Nature Trails

Explore the miles of hiking trails at the Mission Trails Regional Park (www.mtrp.org) and the Torrey Pines State Preserve (see p52). The latter is also prime bird-watching territory. All of San Diego's beaches and parks are great for picnics.

③ Timken Museum of Art

MAP L1 ■ 1500 El Prado, Balboa Park ■ 619 239 5548
■ www.timkenmuseum.org
Admittance is free to this impressive and important collection (see p20) of Russian icons, Parisian tapestries, European Old Masters, American works, and other fine art. The museum's permanent collection includes Bruegel, Rubens, Vermeer, and *Saint Bartholomew* – San Diego's only Rembrandt painting.

Timken Museum of Art

④ Park Life

The city's glorious parks are absolutely free to explore. Centerpiece Balboa Park is by far the urban favorite, while Old Town is full of fascinating history for you to discover. Both Mission Bay Park, with its children's play areas, and the Waterfront Park, with its fun splash fountain, are great for families.

⑤ International Cottages

MAP L1 ■ 1549 El Prado, Balboa Park ■ 619 234 0739
■ Open 11am–5pm Sat & Sun
■ www.sdhpr.org

More than 30 countries are represented within the historic 1935 cottages of Balboa Park's House of Hospitality (see p19). At 2pm, on a rotating basis, member houses epitomize their countries through song, dance, or other means.

⑥ Shakespeare Readings

MAP H5 ■ www.sandiego shakespearesociety.org
Everyone is welcome to join the San Diego Shakespeare Society to participate in or listen with other aficionados to works by the Bard. Visit the website to check out the current schedule of monthly readings and other free events.

7 Walking Tours
619 231 7463
▪ www.walkabout-int.org

Walkabout International leads free tours in and around San Diego. Some walks go through decorated neighborhoods, while others focus on architecture. Standard walks take place in Mission Bay, Shelter Island, Balboa Park, and Mission Hills.

8 Gaze at the Stars
View the night sky at the Reuben H. Fleet Science Center *(see p59)* in Balboa Park. Visitors can star-gaze for free on the first Wednesday of every month, starting at 8pm, through giant telescopes from the San Diego Astronomy Association.

Spreckel's Organ Pavilion

9 Art and Music
Spreckels Organ Society: 619 702 8138; www.spreckelsorgan.org

There are gallery openings most weekends and a monthly art walk at Liberty Station. Free concerts are also held during the year; many take place at beaches and parks throughout summer, including performances by the renowned Spreckels Organ Society. For listings, check www.sandiego.org.

10 59-Mile Scenic Drive
www.sandiego.org

This three-hour drive winds through the city's neighborhoods and offers a plethora of memorable views, from the coastline, the bay, and the downtown skyline, to the bordering mountains, and even Mexico. The drive can also be spread out over several days.

TOP 10 BUDGET TIPS

The free tram in Balboa Park

1 Ride Balboa Park's free daily tram from Inspiration Point parking lot *(www.balboapark.org/visit/parking)* to El Prado attractions.

2 Purchase the Compass Card day or multiday pass *(www.511sd.com/compass)* for easy riding across buses and trolleys.

3 Save money and skip lots of lines at theme parks as well as zoos with CityPass *(www.citypass.com/southern-california)*.

4 Visit many museums and San Diego Zoo with Balboa Park Explorer Pass *(www.explorer.balboapark.org)*.

5 Parking is free on most city side streets, but check signs for time limits.

6 There's free entry to historic structures such as the blacksmith's workshop, mud brick homes, and the museum at Old Town San Diego State Historic Park. You can enjoy a glimpse of life here in the 1800s.

7 Check online site Groupon *(www.groupon.com/local/san-diego)* for deals on dining, attractions, and tours.

8 Published weekly, *San Diego Reader* *(www.sandiegoreader.com)* lists free and cheap events and deals.

9 Pick up half-price theater tickets at the ArtsTix *(www.sdartstix.com)* kiosk in front of the US Grant Hotel in Horton Plaza Park.

10 Join the Morley Field Sports Complex for free or inexpensive sports activities, from jogging and cycling, to archery, basketball, as well as boccie *(www.balboapark.org/in-the-park/morley-field-sports-complex; www.sandiego.gov/park-and-recreation/centers/recctr/morley)*.

Festivals

1 Mardi Gras
Gaslamp Quarter ■ Feb/Mar

Be quick to grab the strings of beads thrown off the floats at the Masquerade Parade. The parade begins in the afternoon at Fifth Avenue, and the music and revelry carry on until the early morning. The food booths serve up New Orleans-style Cajun food.

2 St. Patrick's Day Parade
Mar

A grand parade of marching bands, bagpipes, community organizations, horses, and school groups begins at Sixth and Juniper. Afterward, an Irish festival takes place at Balboa Park with Irish dancers, lots to eat, green beer, and fun for the entire family.

3 Cinco de Mayo
May

North of the Mexican border, commemorating the French defeat by Mexican troops is a serious business. Restaurants overflow, the Old Town State Historic Park sponsors folkloric ballet performances and mariachi bands, and the historic Gaslamp Quarter hosts a musical street fair.

Fireworks marking the Fourth of July

4 Fourth of July Fireworks and Parades
Jul

Nearly every San Diego community has its own July 4th festivities, such as fireworks, surfing contests, parades, and street festivals. Since the ban of home fireworks, commercial firework shows are the way to go. The biggest show in the county is held over San Diego Harbor.

St. Patrick's Day Parade

5 Comic-Con International
Convention Center ■ Late Jul

Comic-Con draws more than 150,000 devotees over several days and literally bursts out of the huge San Diego Convention Center. Tickets sell out super-fast for this wildly popular all-things-comic-and-then-some gathering. Celebrity guests, panels, retailers, games, anime, film screenings, and fringe events line the program.

6 San Diego Pride
Jul

San Diego's LGBTQ+ community hits the streets in celebration of diversity. The iconic parade begins at Fifth Avenue and Laurel in Hillcrest and moves to Balboa Park, where live bands, food booths, and a party atmosphere prevail. Colorful costumes are the rule of the day.

Dancer at Cinco de Mayo celebrations

7 Halloween Festivals & Haunted Houses

Gaslamp Quarter & Balboa Park
■ Oct ■ Adm

Your worst nightmares may come true at the historic 1889 Haunted Hotel, which features ghouls, a clown asylum, and a haunted subway station. The Chamber and Haunted Trails of Balboa Park will terrify you.

8 Mother Goose Parade

El Cajon ■ Sun before Thanksgiving

Floats, equestrian units, and marching bands make up part of the 200 entries in the largest single-day event in San Diego County, attended by about 400,000 people. A tradition since 1947, the parade revolves around a celebration of children.

Mother Goose Parade

9 Christmas on the Prado

Balboa Pk ■ First Fri & Sat of Dec

Balboa Park launches the Christmas season by opening its doors to the community. Museums are free after 5pm, carolers sing, and food booths are set up. The park is closed to traffic, but shuttles reach the outer parking lots. Dress warmly.

10 Boat Parades of Lights

Dec

Yachts and sailboats vie for the title of best decorated in Mission Bay and the San Diego Harbor. The best viewing areas for the Mission Bay parade are at Crown Point and Fiesta Island; for the San Diego Harbor Parade, head to the Embarcadero.

TOP 10 FAIRS AND GATHERINGS

1 Ocean Beach Kite Festival
Ocean Beach ■ Mar
A kite competition with prizes and demonstrations on the beach.

2 Avocado Festival
Fallbrook ■ Apr
Special tours, 50 food booths, and awards for best dishes draw big crowds.

3 Mainly Mozart Festival
Jun ■ Adm
Concerts at San Diego and Tijuana feature works by the wunderkind and his contemporaries.

4 San Diego County Fair
Del Mar ■ Jun ■ Adm
Fairground rides, food, and live music.

5 A Taste of Gaslamp
Gaslamp Quarter ■ Jun ■ Adm
A self-guided tour passes restaurants displaying their kitchen samplings.

6 US Open Sand Castle Competition
Imperial Beach ■ Aug
Competitors build the most complex and imaginative sand castles.

7 Summerfest
Aug
Classical music and modern compositions in La Jolla, with artists and ensembles from around the world.

8 Julian Fall Apple Harvest
Mid-Sep–mid-Oct
Music, apple cider, and apple pies in a charming mountain town.

9 Cabrillo Festival
Cabrillo National Monument ■ End Sep ■ Adm
Soldiers re-enact the Cabrillo landing, and performers showcase Native American, Aztec, and Mexican dances.

10 Fleet Week
Sep/Oct
Navy ship tours and air and sea parades honor the military.

San Diego County Fair performers

San Diego
Area by Area

View across the marina toward the waterfront and its high-rises

TOP 10 Downtown San Diego

Scarcely a generation ago, Downtown San Diego was a downtrodden neighborhood of derelict buildings, until the 1980s urban renewal restored the area's historic cityscape. It has since transformed into a first-class destination for visitors and a trendy area for residents. There are restaurants, art galleries, festivals, centers for performing arts, museums, and a sports stadium. The atmosphere is strictly Southern Californian: a blend of urban energy and laid-back priorities. From the edge of the Embarcadero to the beautifully restored Gaslamp Quarter, downtown is a great place to have fun in.

San Diego Museum of Us in Balboa Park

DOWNTOWN SAN DIEGO

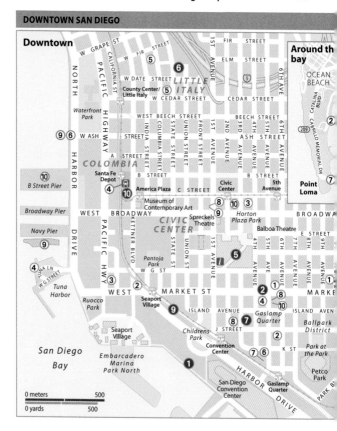

Walkway on the Embarcadero

1 Embarcadero

For those arriving by ship or train, the Embarcadero is San Diego's front door. Passengers disembark from gleaming white cruise ships tied up at B Street Pier

or pass through a 1915 train depot. But the Embarcadero (see pp14–15) is an attraction in itself. Pedestrian-friendly walkways pass historic ships, museums, shopping centers, and parks. Serious and quirky public artworks and a harbor filled with maritime life define this lively district.

2 Gaslamp Quarter

In the mid-19th century, the Gaslamp Quarter (see pp12–13) was the heart of a new city, but within 50 years it had become a much more sordid area filled with gambling halls, opium dens, and brothels, and within another 50 years, it had become a broken-down slum. Restored in the 1980s, it is now a National Historic District. During the day, the gloriously restored buildings attract history buffs and shoppers. By night, crowds dine in fashionable restaurants, listen to music, or sip drinks.

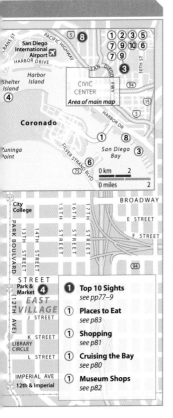

The historic Gaslamp Quarter

3 Balboa Park and San Diego Zoo

Home to the world-famous San Diego Zoo (see p19), 15 unique museums, theaters, recreational opportunities, and exquisite landscaping, Balboa Park (see pp18–21) creates an indelible impression. Year round, vibrant flowers bloom in profusion and pepper tree groves and grassy expanses provide idyllic spots for picnicking. Allow a minimum of a few days to enjoy the park's many attractions.

Central Library, East Village

4 East Village
MAP L5

Formerly a Victorian village that fell into neglect but survived as a warehouse district and artist colony, this area is now very fashionable. Petco Park, home to the San Diego Padres baseball team *(see p55)*, is the neighborhood's major focal point. Check out the 1909 Western Metal Supply building: architects incorporated the vintage building into the stadium's structure. A state-of-the-art Central Library and Children's Museum are located here.

5 The Campus at Horton
MAP J5

Downtown's newest addition replaces Westfield Horton Plaza, a popular former landmark. Though The Campus at Horton, standing ten stories tall, is a shining symbol of contemporary architecture, it does retain some iconic features from the old structure. While it has been built to house offices for life and science technology companies, visitors can enjoy a variety of restaurants, retail shops, wellness facilities, and entertainment venues located here. It is scheduled to open in 2022.

6 Little Italy
MAP J3

This revitalized neighborhood is one of San Diego's oldest. Genoese fishing families were the first Italians to settle along the waterfront in the 1860s. Along with Portuguese immigrants, they founded San Diego's prosperous tuna industry. Little Italy, sometimes known as Middletown, is now a fashionable address. While retaining its Bohemian character, restaurants, galleries, design stores, and a Saturday market line its streets.

7 Asian Pacific Historic District
MAP J5

An eight-block area that overlaps part of the Gaslamp Quarter marks the former center of San Diego's Asian community. Chinese immigrants came to San Diego after the California Gold Rush and found fishing and construction work; others ran opium dens and gambling halls. Japanese and Filipino communities followed. This is the home of Chinese New Year celebrations, a farmers' market, and an Asian bazaar. Join a walking tour at the Chinese Historical Museum *(see p46)*, and admire the Asian architectural flourishes.

8 Marston House
MAP K1 ▪ 3525 7th Ave ▪ 619 297 7511 ▪ Open Sat–Sun for docent-led tours only: half-hourly tours start at 10am; last tour begins at 4pm ▪ Adm

This fine Arts and Crafts house, built in 1905, is open to the public as a

THE FOUNDING OF MODERN SAN DIEGO

When entrepreneur Alonzo Horton arrived in a burgeoning San Diego in 1867, he believed that a new city could prosper in this location. He bought 960 acres and sold and even gave away lots to people. When you walk the Gaslamp Quarter, note the short blocks and lack of alleys, created due to the opinion that corner lots were worth more and alleys only accumulated trash.

museum. The exterior combines elements of Victorian and English Tudor styles, while the interior offers expansive hallways and intimate living spaces adorned with Mission-style furnishings, pottery, paintings, and textiles by craftsman artisans. The museum is operated by the Save Our Heritage Organization.

⑨ Martin Luther King Promenade

MAP H5

Planner Max Schmidt used the idea of functional public art to create this promenade along Harbor Drive. A *serape* of colors, textures, and water-works, the promenade celebrates a multicultural heritage. Granite stones bear quotes by civil-rights leader Dr. Martin Luther King.

Martin Luther King Promenade

⑩ Museum of Contemporary Art

MAP H4 ▪ 1001 & 1100 Kettner Blvd ▪ 858 454 3541 ▪ Open 11am–5pm Thu–Tue (11am–7pm 3rd Thu each month) ▪ Docent-led tours: 5:30pm & 6:45pm 3rd Thu each month, 2pm Sat & Sun (included with admission) ▪ Adm

This two-building downtown location of the museum in La Jolla *(see p34)* presents rotating art exhibits, as well as selected art pieces from the permanent collection. At the entrance is the 18-ft (5.4-m) *Hammering Man at 3,110,527*, a steel and aluminum sculpture by Jonathan Borofsky. The museum also hosts lectures and workshops, and there is a themed gallery tour at the free opening on the third Thursday evening each month.

A DAY WALKING AROUND DOWNTOWN

▶ MORNING

Start at the **Santa Fe Depot** *(see p15)*. Walk right on Broadway, cross the RR tracks, and walk two blocks to Harbor Drive. Turn right and head to the **Maritime Museum of San Diego** *(see p47)*. Check out the exhibits and climb aboard the *Star of India*. Walk back down Harbor Drive to the ticket booth for harbor tours. A narrated harbor cruise brings you close to the naval facilities. Next, spend an hour or so aboard the **USS Midway** at the **USS Midway Museum** *(see pp16–17)*. Finish your morning with lunch at the **Fish Market** *(N. Harbor Dr; 619 232 3474)*.

AFTERNOON

Continue down Harbor Drive to **Seaport Village** *(see p14)* and stay on the sidewalk until you reach a crossing. Turn left; walk up the street past the Manchester Grand Hyatt Hotel, across Harbor Drive and the trolley tracks. Walk onto the **Martin Luther King Promenade**, which stretches past beautiful downtown apartment revitalizations. At the Convention Center trolley stop, turn left, then left again on J St. On J and 3rd, stop by the **San Diego Chinese Historical Museum** *(see p46)*. Turn left on 3rd and right on Island; you'll pass the historic **Horton Grand Hotel** *(see p117)*. At 4th, visit the **William Heath Davis House** *(see p12)*. One block farther is the heart of the **Gaslamp Quarter** *(see pp12–13)*. Pick up a sundae at **Ghirardelli Soda Fountain** *(631 5th St)*.

See map on pp76–7 ←

Cruising the Bay

Aerial view of Coronado Bridge

7 Cabrillo National Monument

Dedicated to the European discovery of San Diego and Alta California, this monument (see p28) draws over one million people a year. The statue of Cabrillo is a replica of an original that could not withstand the wind and salt air.

1 Coronado Bridge

This bridge (see p26) links Coronado to San Diego. Its gradual incline and curve allow cars to maintain speed. It is high enough for aircraft carriers to pass beneath at high tide.

2 SPAWAR
MAP B5

This Navy marine mammal facility trains bottlenose dolphins, with their biological sonar, to locate sea mines.

3 Naval Base San Diego
MAP D6

More than 50 naval ships of the Pacific Fleet are provided with shore support and living quarters by this naval base.

4 Naval Air Station North Island
MAP B5

Several aircraft carriers tie up here. You can often see high-tech aircraft, submarines, and destroyers.

5 Local Marine Wildlife

Seals and sea lions are bay residents. The East Pacific green sea turtle and the California least tern have protected foraging habitats.

6 Naval Amphibious Base

Home to the Navy SEALS and the Navy Parachute Team, the facility (see p26) has served as a training base since 1943. It is responsible for training and maintenance of the ships of the Pacific Fleet.

8 NASSCO Shipyard
MAP D6

The National Steel and Shipbuilding Company designs and builds US Navy auxiliary ships, commercial tankers, and container ships. It is one of the largest shipyards in the US.

9 Museum Vessels of the Embarcadero

The sailing ship *Star of India* dates back to 1863; *Berkeley* used to carry passengers in the Bay Area; and the USS *Midway* features in the USS Midway Museum (see pp15–17).

The *Star of India* on the Embarcadero

10 Cruise Ship Terminal
MAP G4

San Diego boasts the fastest-growing cruise ship port on the west coast, with 180 ships docking at the B Street Pier throughout the year. Cruises leave for excursions to the Mexican Riviera, Hawaii, Canada, the Panama Canal, and the South Pacific.

→ *See map on pp76–7*

Shopping

1 **Goorin Bros. Hat Shop**
MAP K5 ▪ 631 5th Ave ▪ 619 450 6303

Established in 1895, this is the place for serious lovers of quality headgear of all shapes and styles, catering to both men and women.

2 **The Wine Bank**
MAP K6 ▪ 363 5th Ave, Suite 100 ▪ 619 234 7487

Come here *(see p69)* for expert staff and two floors of North American and international wines in all price ranges.

3 **Seaport Village**
MAP H5 ▪ 849 W. Harbor Dr ▪ 619 530 0704 ▪ Open 11am–7pm daily

At this complex *(see p69)* by the bay, you'll find kites, magnets, gifts for left-handed people, and T-shirts galore.

4 **San Diego Trading Company**
MAP K5 ▪ 701 Fifth Ave ▪ 619 458 9001

For San Diego-themed souvenirs, check out the high-quality clothing and novelty items at this store.

5 **Vocabulary**
MAP H3 ▪ 414 W. Cedar St ▪ 619 316 6598

This intimate Little Italy boutique sells apparel for men and women, baby items, home decor, paper goods, and accessories and gifts.

Interior of Vocabulary

6 **Chuck Jones Gallery**
MAP K6 ▪ 232 5th Ave ▪ 949 258 3221

American Pop artworks are on sale here in a gallery setting. Featured artists include Chuck Jones, Dr. Seuss, Charles Schulz, and Tom Everhart.

7 **Spanish Village Art Center**
MAP M1 ▪ 1770 Village Pl ▪ 619 233 9050 ▪ Open 11am–4pm daily

Browse the studios *(see p47)* of more than 200 artists at this center for a unique memento of San Diego.

8 **The Cuban Cigar Factory**
MAP K5 ▪ 551 5th Ave ▪ 619 238 2496

Cigar makers roll tobacco from Central America and the Dominican Republic in San Diego's original cigar factory. Aficionados can select from a variety of cigars.

9 **United Nations International Gift Shop**
MAP L2 ▪ 2171 Pan American Plaza ▪ 619 233 5044

Toys, instruments, jewelry, books, crafts, and ethnic clothing are among the temptations at this colorful store.

10 **Zeglio Custom Clothiers**
MAP J4 ▪ 246 Broadway ▪ 619 343 1433

Custom tailored men's suits, shirts and pants, as well as expert alterations make this the go-to place in San Diego for weddings, special occasions, and style upgrades.

Museum Shops

Jewelry at the Museum of Art shop

1 San Diego Museum of Art

Exhibit-led art books, toys, stationery, jewelry, purses and flower pressing kits and many other items are sold here *(see p20)*.

2 Mingei International Museum

This museum *(see p20)* store is filled with ethnic clothes, Chinese brushes, Russian dolls, chiming bells, and a good selection of *alebrijes* (Mexican folk art sculptures).

3 San Diego Museum of Us

Crafts from around Latin America here *(see p20)* include Peruvian gourds, Mexican folk art, and three-legged Chilean good luck pigs. There is also a wide range of Native American crafts such as silver jewelry.

4 Museum of Contemporary Art

Check out the select merchandise that relates to the museum's *(see p79)* special exhibitions. The latest art books and handcrafted jewelry are always on offer.

5 San Diego Art Institute Shop

MAP L1 ■ House of Charm, Balboa Pk
Juried art shows present the work of local artists, whose works often go on sale after being exhibited. This small shop features glass sculptures, porcelain *objets d'art*, hand-painted cushions, and jewelry.

6 Maritime Museum of San Diego

Gratify your nautical gift needs with a variety of model ships, T-shirts, posters, and prints inscribed with an image of the *Star of India (see p47)*.

7 Reuben H. Fleet Science Center

Science toys, videos, puzzles, and hands-on games here *(see p59)* are very popular with the kids.

8 San Diego Chinese Historical Museum

Chinese calligraphy sets, tea sets, snuff bottles, and chops – a type of carved stamp used to sign one's name – are on sale here *(see p46)*.

Store at Museum of Photographic Arts

9 Museum of Photographic Arts

Exhibition catalogs, prints, note cards, and calendars represent the world's finest photographic artists *(see p20)*, both past and present. A wide range of books is also available.

10 San Diego History Center

If you're interested in San Diego's past, including haunted locations and biographies, this museum *(see p20)* offers one of the best collections of local history books.

Places to Eat

PRICE CATEGORIES

Price categories include a three-course meal for one, half a bottle of wine, and all unavoidable extra charges including tax.

$ under $40 $$ $40–$80 $$$ over $80

1 Cowboy Star Restaurant and Butcher Shop

MAP K5 ▪ 640 10th Ave ▪ 619 450 5880 ▪ $$$

With an Old West ambience, this stylish restaurant serves some of the finest hand-cut steaks in San Diego along with specialty cocktails.

2 Kansas City Barbeque

MAP H5 ▪ 600 W. Harbor Dr ▪ 619 231 9680 ▪ $

This restaurant shot to fame as a setting in the iconic film *Top Gun*. It serves big plates of barbecue favorites with traditional sides.

3 The Grant Grill

MAP J4 ▪ US Grant Hotel, 326 Broadway ▪ 619 744 2077 ▪ $$

With a club-like ambience, The Grant Grill offers contemporary California cuisine. Try the famous mock turtle soup with chervil and sherry.

4 Top of the Market

MAP G5 ▪ 750 N. Harbor Dr ▪ 619 234 4867 ▪ $$$

Chichi restaurant with fabulous views. Come here for a calm atmosphere, and delicious seafood.

5 Filippi's Pizza Grotto

MAP H3 ▪ 1747 India St ▪ 619 232 5095 ▪ $

One of the city's most-loved local Italian spots *(see p66)*. Guests should expect a wait as there is limited seating here.

6 The Prado at Balboa Park

MAP L1 ▪ 1549 El Prado, Balboa Pk ▪ 619 557 9441 ▪ $$

Made with *tres leches* (sponge soaked in three types of milk), caramelized banana, meringue, and fired plantain, the Prado Tres Leches is a must try here *(see p67)*.

7 Lou & Mickey's

MAP J6 ▪ 224 5th Ave ▪ 619 237 4900 ▪ $$$

Delectable steaks, fresh seafood, and pasta dishes are served at booths, tables, or on a shaded patio.

Patio area at Lou & Mickey's

8 Tender Greens

MAP J4 ▪ 110 W. Broadway ▪ 619 795 2353 ▪ $

There's something for everyone here – from fried chicken and hearty salads, to vegan options and soups.

9 Currant Brasserie

MAP J4 ▪ 140 W. Broadway ▪ 619 702 6309 ▪ $

American and French classics such as skillet breakfasts, New Orleans-style beignets, juicy burgers and an absinthe menu draw locals in a steady stream.

10 Rustic Root

MAP K5 ▪ 535 5th Ave ▪ 619 232 1747 ▪ $$

Head to this rooftop restaurant for a taste of New American comfort food with California accents and unrivalled views of the Gaslamp Quarter.

See map on pp76–7

TOP 10 Old Town, Uptown, and Mission Valley

This long stretch follows the San Diego River from the Mission San Diego de Alcalá to Old Town. For as long as 12,000 years, the Kumeyaay tribe lived in small settlements in the valley – hunting, gathering, and growing crops. In 1769, Spanish soldiers and Franciscan padres arrived in the area, followed by San Diego's first Spanish settlers. The valley itself holds little of interest beyond masses of chain motels and shopping centers intersected by a freeway; however, on the bluffs above, you'll find eclectic neighborhoods overflowing with charm, brilliant architecture, and chic restaurants. Tolerance and diversity create a progressive, alternative air, while rising real estate prices have turned simple bungalow homes into showpieces. And San Diego's birthplace is always close by.

Mormon Battalion Memorial

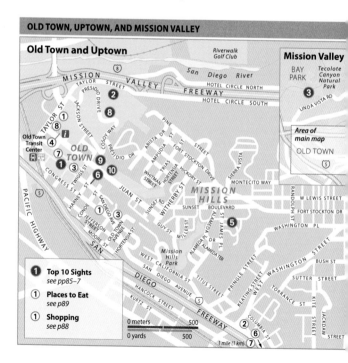

OLD TOWN, UPTOWN, AND MISSION VALLEY

Old Town and Uptown

Mission Valley

① Top 10 Sights
see pp85–7

① Places to Eat
see p89

① Shopping
see p88

0 meters 500
0 yards 500
1 mile (1 km)

1 Old Town State Historic Park

San Diego's first commercial settlement (see pp24–5) has been either preserved or re-created in this pedestrian-only park. Much of the town was destroyed in a fire in 1872, prompting the development of a new town center closer to the water, but several original structures remain. You can wander into any of Old Town's houses and find museums or concession shops inside.

2 Junípero Serra Museum

MAP P4 ▪ 2727 Presidio Dr ▪ 619 232 6203 ▪ Hours vary, check website ▪ Adm ▪ www.sandiego history.org

Constructed in 1929 to a design by William Templeton Johnson, the museum building is in keeping with the city's Spanish-Colonial heritage. Its white stucco arches, narrow passages, red-tile roof, and stately tower pay tribute to the first mission, which stood near this site. Artifacts from ongoing archeological excavations, ceramics made by the Kumeyaay tribe, clothing, furniture, and a cannon help illustrate the simple life people led. Climb the tower to compare today's view with that of 1929.

3 University of San Diego

MAP C4 ▪ 5998 Alcalá Park ▪ 619 260 4600

Grand Spanish Renaissance buildings distinguish this independent Catholic university, its design inspired by the university in the Spanish town of Alcalá de Henares. Of exceptional note is the Founders Chapel with its white marble altar, gold-leaf decoration, 14 stained-glass nave windows, and marble floor.

University of San Diego

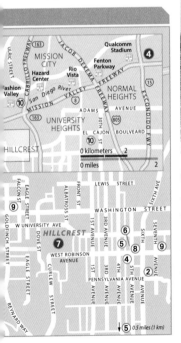

4 Mission Basilica San Diego de Alcalá

A peaceful enclave among the nondescript strip malls of Mission Valley, the mission's (see pp30–31) original spirit still lingers in the church and its lovely gardens. The first of California's 21 missions was moved to this permanent site a few years after its founding. Over time, the structure was rebuilt to suit the needs of the time. Its famous facade and bell tower have inspired architects to copy the "Mission Style" throughout San Diego.

5 Mission Hills
MAP Q5 ▪ Mission Hills
Nursery: 1525 Fort Stockton Dr

One of San Diego's most charming and romantic neighborhoods is in the hills overlooking Old Town and San Diego Bay. Tree-lined streets run past architectural jewels built by some of the city's leading architects in various styles, including Craftsman and Prairie School. When they were first constructed in the early 1900s, homes had to cost at least $3,500. Kate Sessions' 1910 nursery (see p21) can still be visited here.

Interior of haunted Whaley House

6 Whaley House Museum
MAP P5 ▪ 2476 San Diego Ave ▪ 619 297 7511 ▪ Open 10am–4:30pm daily; nighttime ghost tours available, call to confirm seasonal times ▪ Adm ▪ www.whaleyhouse.org

California's first two-story brick structure also served as San Diego's first courthouse, county seat, and home to Thomas Whaley, who built it in 1856 over a graveyard and site of a former gallows. The US Commerce Department declared the house officially haunted in the 1960s.

7 Hillcrest
MAP C4

Considered San Diego's first suburb in the 1920s, Hillcrest slowly developed into a residential area, offering a quiet alternative to the bustle of downtown. A trolley stop opened the neighborhood up to thriving businesses, restaurants, and theaters; in the 1940s, merchants

APOLINARIA LORENZANA

In 1800, Apolinaria Lorenzana and 20 orphans arrived from Mexico to be distributed to respectable presidio families. She taught herself to write by copying every written thing she found. She spent her life caring for the mission padres, teaching children and women church doctrine, and tending the sick. Nicknamed La Beata, she was one of the few women to receive a land grant.

proudly erected a sign that spanned University Boulevard, proclaiming "Hillcrest" to the world. But fortunes changed, neglect followed, and this sign came down. In the 1970s, the LGBTQ+ community took up the revitalization challenge and trans-formed the community into a hip destination with great restaurants, nightlife, and avant-garde shops. And now the sign is back – in neon.

8 Presidio Park
MAP P5

The Kumeyaay tribe once used this hillside for sacred ceremonies. Site of the original Spanish presidio and mission settlement, a lovely park is all that's left of San Diego's beginnings. The park contains the Junípero Serra Museum (see p85) and the remaining earthen walls of Fort Stockton, a fortress that changed hands several times during the Mexican-American War, marked by bronze monuments, a flagpole, and a cannon. The 28-ft (8.5-m)

Serra Cross, constructed from mission tiles, honors founder Saint Junípero Serra *(see p30)*.

9 Mormon Battalion Memorial Visitor's Center

MAP P5 ▪ 2510 Juan St ▪ 619 298 3317 ▪ Open 10am–7pm Mon, Wed–Sat, 5–7pm Tue, 1–7pm Sun

In July 1846, 500 men, 32 women, and 51 children set out from Council Bluffs, Iowa, on what would be considered one of the longest military marches in history. Six months and 2,000 miles (3,218 km) later, they reached San Diego to support the American military garrison in the Mexican-American War. At the Visitor's Center, a volunteer from the Church of Latter-Day Saints discusses the march and Mormon contributions to the area.

10 Heritage Park

MAP P5 ▪ County 2454 Heritage Park Row ▪ 858 565 3600 ▪ Open 9am–5pm daily

Downtown's rapid expansion after World War II almost destroyed several Victorian heritage houses and San Diego's first synagogue. The Save Our Heritage Organization rescued and moved these architectural treasures to this specially created park. Of notable interest is the Sherman Gilbert House, once home to art and music patrons Bess and Gertrude Gilbert, who hosted luminaries such as Artur Rubinstein and Anna Pavlova.

Houses in Heritage Park

A WALK AROUND OLD TOWN, HERITAGE PARK, AND PRESIDIO PARK

▶ MORNING

Begin at the Old Town Transit Center. Cross the street and follow the path into **Old Town State Historic Park** *(see p85)*. Just to the left is the Interpretive Center, where you can pick up a map. Walk along the right side of the Plaza and peek into the Bailey & McGuire Pottery Shop. Follow the signs to **La Casa de Machado y Stewart** *(see p25)* and the **Mason Street School** *(see p24)*. Back at the Plaza, visit **La Casa de Estudillo** *(see p24)* for the best insight into an upper-class home of early California. From the Plaza's southwest corner, continue out of the State Park. Walk along San Diego Avenue, where you'll find souvenir shops, galleries, and restaurants. Try the **Old Town Mexican Café** *(see p89)* for lunch.

AFTERNOON

Cross the street at Conde and backtrack up San Diego Avenue to visit the haunted **Whaley House**. Turn right on Harney Street and walk uphill to **Heritage Park**. Backtrack one block to the **Mormon Battalion Visitor's Center**. Turn right on Juan Street and walk to Mason. You'll see a sign indicating "The Old Presidio Historic Trail." Turn right on Mason, follow the golf course to Jackson, and look for the footpath across the street. You'll parallel Jackson to the left and wind uphill to **Presidio Park**. Across the grass are the ruins of **Serra Cross**, the original presidio, and the **Junípero Serra Museum** *(see p85)*.

See map on pp84–5 ←

Shopping

1 Bazaar del Mundo
MAP N5 ▪ 4133 Taylor St
▪ 619 296 3161

In a lushly landscaped plaza, quality shops offer Mexican tableware, folk art, Guatemalan textiles, and books.

2 Gioia's Room
MAP C4 ▪ 3739 6th Ave
▪ 619 431 5723

An interesting boutique that offers accessories and vintage women's clothing with free alterations.

3 Old Town Market
MAP N5 ▪ 4010 Twiggs St
▪ 619 278 0955

This festive market offers entertainment and works by local artisans. The shops sell colorful Mexican goods, such as Day of the Dead folk art, as well as jewelry and gifts.

Mexican crucifixes, Old Town Market

4 Trillion Jewels
MAP N5 ▪ 2802 Juan St
▪ 760 828 8683

A fun stop to search for out-of-the-ordinary jewelry, this Old Town shop has an amazing range of gemstones, including new, vintage, and antique pieces.

5 Record City
MAP C4 ▪ 3757 6th Ave
▪ 619 291 5313

There's nothing quite like vinyl, and the crates here are stocked with rock and 1980s and 1990s alternative music. Used CDs are also on sale.

6 Thread & Seed
MAP J1 ▪ 2870 4th Ave
▪ 619 994 1425

This small, tidy and elegant shop features luxe bath products, cosmetics, candles, chocolates, books and jewelry. Their custom gift boxes are a specialty.

7 Geppetto's
MAP N5 ▪ 2754 Calhoun St
▪ 619 293 7520

With a large selection of educational and classic toys and games, this family-owned store is the perfect place to find imaginative gifts for kids of all ages.

8 Bluestocking Books
MAP C4 ▪ 3817 5th Ave
▪ 619 296 1424

This independent store offers new and used books on a wide range of subjects. The search service aims to locate rare and vintage items.

9 Whole Foods
MAP C4 ▪ 711 University Ave
▪ 619 294 2800

With an emphasis on fresh organic food, you'll find flavorful produce, a great assortment of imported goods, and a deli that specializes in healthy takeout.

10 Fashion Valley
MAP C4 ▪ 7007 Friars Rd
▪ 619 297 3381

From Neiman Marcus and Nordstrom to Apple, Gucci, and Tiffany, this two- level, open-air mall *(see p68)* has more than 200 stores. There are also many great food outlets and an 18-screen theater. The mall closes at 9pm every night.

Places to Eat

1. Jack and Giulio's Italian Restaurant

MAP P5 ▪ 2391 San Diego Ave ▪ 619 294 2074 ▪ $$

Classics like Caprese salad and scampi are served in a romantic and intimate space – a welcome respite from the crowds in Old Town.

Thai dishes are served up at Saffron

2. Saffron

MAP C4 ▪ 3737 India St ▪ 619 574 7737 ▪ $

Parking is tricky, but crowds come here for wondrously flavorful Thai cuisine. Takeout is also available.

3. El Agave Tequileria

MAP P6 ▪ 2304 San Diego Ave ▪ 619 220 0692 ▪ $$

Utter culinary magic awaits within one of the first tequilarias in San Diego. Classic Mexican food with modern touches.

4. Crest Café

MAP C4 ▪ 425 Robinson Ave ▪ 619 295 2510 ▪ $

Locals love this upscale diner, serving fresh soups, salads, and big burgers.

Dessert at Crest Café

5. Arriverderci Ristorante

MAP C4 ▪ 3845 4th Ave ▪ 619 299 6282 ▪ $$

Service at this cozy spot is friendly, prices are reasonable, and the pasta dishes are some of the best in town.

PRICE CATEGORIES
Price categories include a three-course meal for one, half a bottle of wine, and all unavoidable extra charges including tax.

$ under $40 $$ $40–$80 $$$ over $80

---

6. Blue Water Seafood Market & Grill

MAP C4 ▪ 3667 India St ▪ 619 497 0914 ▪ $

A fabulous selection of seafood is on offer at this friendly seafood market. Try the fish tacos, seafood cocktails, or chowders.

7. Bertrand at Mr. A's

MAP J1 ▪ 2550 5th Ave, 12th Floor ▪ 619 239 1377 ▪ $$

Popular choices at Bertrand at Mr. A's (see p66) include sautéed Alaskan halibut with scallops and a trio of scrumptious vegetarian creations.

8. Casa Guadalajara

MAP N5 ▪ 4105 Taylor St ▪ 619 295 5111 ▪ $$

This festive restaurant is a grand celebration of Mexican specialties and premium margaritas, along with folk art, fountains, and mariachis.

9. Farmer's Bottega

MAP C4 ▪ 860 W. Washington St ▪ 619 458 9929 ▪ $$

In a rustic farmhouse setting, this restaurant serves seasonal farm-to-table fare. The short rib is a firm favorite.

10. San Diego Chicken Pie Shop

MAP D4 ▪ 2633 El Cajon, North Park ▪ 619 295 0156 ▪ No credit cards ▪ $

Seniors and budget-eaters love the hearty food here: think tasty chicken pies accompanied by mashed potatoes and gravy.

See map on pp84–5 »

🔟 Ocean Beach, Coronado, and the South

West of the center lie two oceanside neighborhoods: Coronado and Ocean Beach, both offering excellent shopping, dining, and sandy shores. In the areas south of San Diego, towards the Mexican border many Mexican citizens live, work, and send their children to school; here the blend of cultures is very evident. While Americans used to enjoy day trips to Tijuana, the specter of drug-cartel violence has made many more cautious.

Point Loma

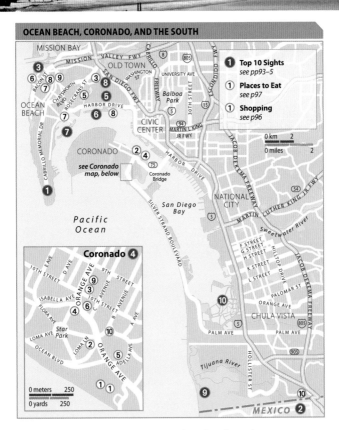

OCEAN BEACH, CORONADO, AND THE SOUTH

1 **Top 10 Sights** see pp93–5

1 **Places to Eat** see p97

1 **Shopping** see p96

Previous pages The Botanical Building and the Lily Pond in Balboa Park

1 Point Loma

Over one million people a year visit the Cabrillo National Monument at Point Loma (see pp28–9). The views are mesmerizing, and the peninsula ends at the meeting point of the Pacific Ocean and San Diego Bay. Half the peninsula is occupied by the military, preventing overdevelopment. Spend time at Sunset Cliffs Park and perhaps spot a whale.

2 Tijuana

During the days of Prohibition, Tijuana, Mexico, used to be the destination of choice for the Hollywood elite and their followers, and for alcohol and gambling. The palatial, Moorish-designed Agua Caliente Casino & Spa was so popular that it had its own landing airstrip for private planes. Fortunes fell when Mexico declared casino gambling illegal in 1935, and the city later reinvented itself as a shopping and dining tourist destination. In recent years, however, drug cartel violence has escalated, and visitors should be diligent and heed all published government warnings.

3 Ocean Beach

Unconventional and laid-back, OB, as it's locally known, has a somewhat hippie-like feel. On main thoroughfare Newport Avenue, you can still find a few original shops. But OB is mainly about the beach: on any day of the year, surfers are waiting for the next swell; volleyball players are spiking balls over the net; and dogs are running freely on Dog Beach (see p49).

The famous Hotel del Coronado

4 Coronado

In the 1880s, two wealthy businessmen, Elisha Babcock, Jr. and Hampton Story, purchased Coronado (see pp26–7) and set out to build a town. They sold lots, laid streets, and constructed the landmark Hotel del Coronado (see p26). John D. Spreckels (see p41) soon bought them out and turned Coronado into a haven for old-money gentry. The military permanently took over much of the peninsula during World War I. The old mansions, resorts, and military base exist harmoniously and give Coronado its unique identity.

5 San Diego International Airport

MAP G2

No matter where you are in San Diego, look up and you'll see a jet soaring dramatically past the downtown high-rises on its final approach to Lindbergh Field (see p42). One hundred years ago, this area was a muddy wasteland that proved to be an ideal spot for budding inventors and pilots to try out their latest machines. In 1927, Ryan Aviation designed, produced, and tested on the beach the *Spirit of St. Louis*, the historic plane that Charles Lindbergh piloted solo across the Atlantic.

Surfer at Ocean Beach

Boats moored in the marina at Harbor Island

6 Harbor Island
MAP C5

Created from 3.5 million tons of mud from the bottom of San Diego Bay, this recreational island is a peninsula that extends into the bay south from the airport. Hotels, restaurants, and marinas offer gorgeous views across the bay of downtown, Point Loma, and Coronado. Facing the island is Spanish Landing Park: commemorating the 1769 meeting of the sea and land expeditions of Gaspar de Portolá and Junípero Serra *(see p40)*. It is dotted with public art and picnic tables, and lined with a sandy beach.

Shoreline Park on Shelter Island

7 Shelter Island
MAP B5

Not really an island but a peninsula that juts out into San Diego Bay from Point Loma, this is home to pleasure boats and a park along its length. In the 1950s, the city dredged millions of tons of sand and mud from the bay onto a sandbar to create land for

marinas and hotels. A number of hotels still have hints of Polynesian themes, a popular style at the time. The San Diego Yacht Club here is the three-time host of the prestigious America's Cup sailing race.

8 Marine Corps Recruit Depot
MAP B5 ▪ 1600 Henderson Ave ▪ 619 524 6719 ▪ Open 8:30am–4pm Mon–Sat (photo ID for Depot; proof of insurance if driving)

Listed on the National Register of Historic Places, the quaint Spanish-Colonial buildings were designed by Bertram Goodhue, architect of several buildings for the Panama-California Exposition in Balboa Park *(see pp18–19)*. The Command Museum displays the history of the

TENT CITY

When John D. Spreckels acquired the Hotel del Coronado in 1890, he felt the beauty of the area should be available to everyone. He built "Tent City," a makeshift town that catered to the less-well-to-do. Arriving by rail and car, families paid $4.50 a week to live in tents equipped with beds, dressers, and flush toilets. Amenities included carnival booths, Japanese gardens, a library, and children's activities. At its peak, the town held 10,000 visitors. The tents came down by 1939, when they could no longer compete with the rising popularity of the roadside motel.

Marine Corps in Southern California and the wars in which they fought. Exhibits include photos, training films, and a World War II ambulance.

9 Border Field State Park

Found within the Tijuana River National Estuarine Research Reserve *(see p53)*, this state park consists of a number of different coastal habitats, such as salt marshes and sand dunes. It's an important habitat for endangered birds, including the California Least Tern and Western snowy plover. Visitors come here to hike, picnic on the beach, and bird-watch. A giant metal fence, which separates the US and Mexico, slices through the park *(see p43)* before plunging into the sea. Swimming in the sea is not recommended due to dangerous currents and an absence of lifeguards. The park can also flood on occasion.

Owl, Living Coast Discovery Center

10 Living Coast Discovery Center

MAP E3 ■ 1000 Gunpowder Point, Chula Vista ■ 619 409 5900 ■ Open 10am–5pm daily ■ Adm

The center is in the Sweetwater Marsh National Wildlife Refuge, one of the few accessible salt marshes left on the Pacific Coast. Rent some binoculars and climb to an observation deck to spot several of the 200 species of birds in the refuge. Or take a self-guided tour along interpretative trails. Children can go on wildlife tours to see raptors, sea turtles, and bat rays up close. The parking lot is located near the Baysite/E Street Trolley Station; a free shuttle will take you to the center.

A BIKE RIDE AROUND CORONADO

▶ **MORNING**

Begin at **Bikes & Beyond** *(see p54)* at the **Ferry Landing Market Place** *(see p26)*. Walk to the sidewalk facing the harbor and enjoy the city view. Pedestrians and joggers also use this sidewalk, so proceed cautiously. Around the corner, you will face the **Coronado Bridge** *(see p26)*; the bougainvillea-covered walls on the right mark the **Marriott Resort** *(see p116)*. Information boards on the way depict harbor wildlife and a map indicates the various navy yards. Under the bridge, the path turns away from the water. At the street, bear left and cross over. There is no protected bike path, but traffic is light on Glorietta Blvd.

At the marina, the road will fork; take the lower road to the left. Turn right at the stop-light and get off your bike; bike riding is forbidden on Orange Avenue. **Moo Time Creamery** *(1025 Orange Ave)* serves delicious homemade ice cream and smoothies. Walk your bike back to the **Hotel del Coronado** *(see p26)* and check out the shops on its lower level *(see p96)*. Leaving the hotel, bear left to Ocean Avenue; the Pacific Ocean is on the left and several mansions, built in the 1900s–1920s, are on the right. Turn right on Alameda and ride through a typical Coronado neighborhood with Spanish-style houses and bungalows. At 4th, cross the street and walk one block; the **Naval Air Station** *(see p80)* will be on your left. Turn right on 1st. It's a straight stretch back to the Market Place.

See map on p92 ←

Shopping

 Shops at the Hotel del Coronado

You'll find some of the best shopping in Coronado among these extensive shops in the hotel *(see p26)*, including women's upscale casual wear, sunglasses, toys, jewelry, and the books of L. Frank Baum.

Ferry Landing Marketplace

2 Ferry Landing Marketplace

MAP C6

Next to the Coronado Ferry dock *(see p27)*, this place offers an eclectic selection of souvenirs, clothing, and galleries. A great farmers' market sets up on Tuesday afternoons.

3 Bookstar/Loma Theatre
MAP B4 ■ 3150 Rosecrans Place ■ 619 225 0465

Barnes & Noble's branded store Bookstar is set in the vintage Loma Theatre, with its original facade, and makes for a special experience.

4 Coronado Museum of History and Art Store

Head to this museum *(see pp26–7)* store for historic photos, posters, and books, as well as a fun selection of *Wizard of Oz*-themed gifts – author L. Frank Baum lived in Coronado.

5 Liberty Station
MAP B5 ■ 2640 Historic Decatur ■ 619 573 9300

You'll find exciting art stores, grocers, wine shops, bakeries, chocolatiers, ethnic jewelry, and more at this waterfront market location *(see p68)*. Entertainment events are also held frequently.

6 Bay Books
MAP C6 ■ 1007 Orange Ave, Coronado ■ 619 435 0070

This independent bookstore has helpful staff, an ample selection of books of local interest and international papers and magazines.

7 Newport Avenue
MAP B4 ■ Ocean Beach

The main drag through Ocean Beach is chock full of antique shops. Some doorways front malls with dozens of shops inside. Finds range from 1950s retro pieces to Victorian and Asian antiques.

8 Ocean Beach People's Organic Food Market
MAP B4 ■ 4765 Voltaire St ■ 619 224 1387

This co-op market has been selling organic, minimally processed natural foods since 1971. For food to go, try the upstairs vegan deli. Non-members are welcome but will be charged a small percentage more.

9 Blue Jeans and Bikinis
MAP C6 ■ 971 Orange Ave, Coronado ■ 619 319 5858

The trendiest blue jeans, along with a wide selection of bikinis, boots, and accessories, are all part of the changing inventory here.

10 Las Americas Premium Outlets
MAP E3 ■ 4211 Camino de la Plaza

Within walking distance of the border with Mexico, you can stop by this *(see p114)* immense 560,000-sq-ft (52,000-sq-m) outlet center.

See map on p92

Places to Eat

 Seréa
MAP C6 ■ Hotel del Coronado,
1500 Orange Ave ■ 619 522 8100
■ $$$

At this elegant restaurant,
sustainable fresh-catch seafood
is complemented with seasonal
produce and an eclectic wine list.

 Chez Loma
MAP C6 ■ 1132 Loma Ave,
Coronado ■ 619 435 0661 ■ Closed
Mon ■ $$

The luscious French cuisine will put
you in heaven. Diners can get great-
value meals in the early-bird special.

 Clayton's Coffee Shop
MAP C6 ■ 979 Orange
Ave ■ 619 435 5425 ■ No credit
cards ■ $

Come here for home-style cooking.
A quarter buys three jukebox plays.

4 **Il Fornaio**
MAP C6 ■ 1333 First St,
Coronado ■ 619 437 4911 ■ $$

Homemade pasta, pizza, and gnocchi,
as well as authentic Italian specialties,
are served at this waterfront joint.

5 **Miguel's Cocina**
MAP C6 ■ 1351 Orange Ave,
Coronado ■ 619 437 4237 ■ $$

Colorfully dressed waitstaff serve
up enormous plates and lethal
margaritas. The enchiladas, tacos,
and burritos are delicious.

Outdoor patio at Miguel's Cocina

PRICE CATEGORIES
Price categories include a three-course
meal for one, half a bottle of wine, and all
unavoidable extra charges including tax.

$ under $40 $$ $40–$80 $$$ over $80

 Hodad's
MAP A4 ■ 5010 Newport Ave
■ 619 224 4623 ■ $

Soak up the "junkyard Gothic"
ambience at this beach café devoted
to burgers, brews, and surf.

 Point Loma Seafoods
MAP B5 ■ 2805 Emerson St
■ 619 223 1109 ■ $

Order the freshest seafood in San
Diego. Salads and sushi are popular.

8 **Island Prime**
MAP C5 ■ 880 Harbor Island
Dr ■ 619 298 6802 ■ $$$

With its waterfront view and
excellent service, this is a pre-
ferred spot for special occasions.

9 **Peace Pies**
MAP B4 ■ 4230 Voltaire St
■ 619 223 2880 ■ $

Pick up picnic fare or eat in the small
dining area or on the outdoor patio.
All choices are vegan and gluten free.

10 **Lobster West**
MAP C6 ■ 1033 B Ave,
Coronado ■ 619 675 0002 ■ $

Fresh Maine lobster is shipped
overnight for the delicious lobster
rolls, creamy bisque, and the salads.

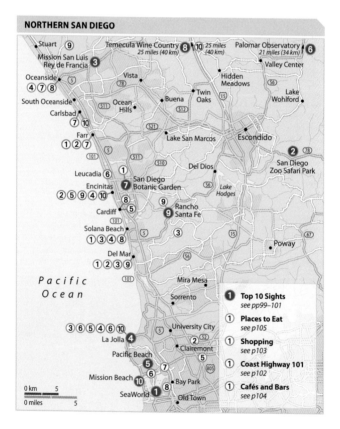 Northern San Diego

San Diego's explosive growth has been concentrated in North County, formerly an area of wide-open spaces. Prosperous hi-tech, biotech, commercial, and financial businesses have relocated here and play a major role in the city's development. Over one million people live in communities with distinct identities, from the high-end rural estates of Rancho Santa Fe to the more modest housing of Marine Corps families in Oceanside. Travel through fabled beach resorts into laid-back surfer towns and active Camp Pendleton Marine Base, or head east from Oceanside past flower farms and avocado groves, filled with blooms and fruit.

Fountain in the San Diego Botanic Garden

NORTHERN SAN DIEGO

- Stuart (9)
- Mission San Luis Rey de Francia (3)
- Oceanside (4)(7)(8)
- South Oceanside
- Carlsbad
- Farr (1)(2)(7)
- Leucadia (6)
- Encinitas (2)(5)(9)(4)(10)
- Cardiff
- Solana Beach (1)(3)(4)(8)
- Del Mar (1)(2)(3)(9)

- Temecula Wine Country (8) (10) 25 miles (40 km)
- Vista (78)
- Ocean Hills (511)
- Buena
- Twin Oaks (S12)
- Lake San Marcos (S10)
- Del Dios
- San Diego Botanic Garden (7)
- Rancho Santa Fe (9)

- Palomar Observatory 21 miles (34 km) (6)
- Valley Center
- Hidden Meadows
- Lake Wohlford
- Escondido
- San Diego Zoo Safari Park (2) (78)
- Lake Hodges
- Poway (67)

- Mira Mesa
- Sorrento
- University City
- Clairemont (52)
- La Jolla (3)(6)(5)(4)(6)(10) (4)
- Pacific Beach (5)
- Mission Beach (10)
- Bay Park
- SeaWorld (1)
- Old Town

Pacific Ocean

0 km 5
0 miles 5

(1)	**Top 10 Sights** *see pp99–101*
(1)	**Places to Eat** *see p105*
(1)	**Shopping** *see p103*
(1)	**Coast Highway 101** *see p102*
(1)	**Cafés and Bars** *see p104*

1 SeaWorld

MAP B4 ▪ 500 Sea World Dr, Mission Bay ▪ 619 222 4732 ▪ Open daily ▪ Adm (special prices online) ▪ www.seaworld.com/sandiego

Opened in 1964, SeaWorld covers 150 acres (60 ha) of Mission Bay and allows visitors to see many ocean creatures up close, including playful penguins, sea otters, walruses, and seals. The family-oriented thrill rides found here can compete with those of most adventure parks. It also has a rescue and rehabilitation program for stranded marine animals. However, less positive aspects of SeaWorld have come to light since the release of the 2013 documentary *Blackfish*.

2 San Diego Zoo Safari Park

MAP E2 ▪ 15500 San Pasqual Valley Rd, Escondido ▪ 619 231 1515 ▪ Open 9am–5pm daily (mid-Jun–mid-Sep & mid-to end Dec: to 7pm) ▪ Adm

Many people prefer the Zoo Safari Park to its sister zoo in Balboa Park (see p19). By monorail, zipline, or a range of safaris, experience African and Asian animals roaming freely in enormous enclosures. Don't miss the Tull Family Tiger Trail, which takes you up close to Sumatran tigers. A successful breeding program works with more than 165 endangered species, including rhinos and lions.

3 Mission San Luis Rey de Francia

MAP D1 ▪ 4050 Mission Ave, Oceanside ▪ 760 757 3651 (ext. 117) ▪ Open 10am–5pm daily ▪ Adm ▪ www.sanluisrey.org

Named after canonized French king Louis IX, this mission was the last established in Southern California.

It was built largely by members of the Payomkowishum, a local Native American tribe, who had been converted to Christianity. After a period of disrepair, the mission was restored in the late 19th century. It has an elegant exterior with Roman arches, and a striking church with a domed bell tower. Inside there are displays on life during the mission era. The mission also offers popular retreats.

Mission San Luis Rey de Francia

4 La Jolla

Surrounded on three sides by ocean bluffs and beaches boasting spectacular views, this gorgeous enclave (see p35) is noted for upscale shops, boutiques, and fine-dining restaurants. Often cited as having the most expensive properties in the country, it is also home to several prestigious educational and research facilities (see p100). Torrey Pines offers a number of hiking trails and the famous Torrey Pines Golf Course.

La Jolla cove

5 Pacific Beach
MAP A3

Residents here enjoy an endless summer climate and easy-going lifestyle. Life revolves around Garnet Avenue's nightclubs, cafés, late-night restaurants, and shops. The street ends at the 1927 Crystal Pier, a great spot to see surfers, or spend a night in a tiny cottage. Come early to claim a fire ring on the beach and cook up some marshmallows, or cycle the boardwalk to Mission Beach *(see p49)*.

BRAIN POWER

Beneath San Diego's "fun in the sun" image is one of the country's most educated populations. With one of the nation's highest incidences of PhDs per capita, 30 percent of residents hold college degrees, and 20 percent of adults are in higher education. La Jolla boasts some of the most prestigious research facilities: the Salk Institute, Scripps Research Institute, Scripps Institution of Oceanography, and UC San Diego.

Hale Telescope, Palomar Observatory

6 Palomar Observatory
MAP E1 ■ 35899 Canfield Rd, Palomar Mountain ■ 760 742 2119 ■ Open 9am–3pm daily (to 4pm Apr–Oct)

Atop one of North County's highest mountains, the dome of the observatory has an otherworldly look. Part of the California Institute of Technology, Palomar is home to the 200-in (508-cm) Hale Telescope, the largest optical instrument of its kind when installed in 1947. Its moving parts weigh 530 tons, the mirror 14.5 tons. Thanks to computer technology, no one "looks" through the telescope anymore. Self-guided tours offer a look at the telescope itself.

7 San Diego Botanic Garden
MAP D2 ■ 230 Quail Gardens Dr, Encinitas ■ 760 436 3036 ■ Open 9am–5pm Wed–Sun (exc. Christmas Day) ■ Adm

This is a treasure-packed expanse of nearly two dozen gardens on well-marked pathways, with viewpoints, sculpture exhibits, garden shops, and plenty of opportunities for bird-watching. Dedicated areas display Australian, African, Mexican, and Central American gardens; succulents and dragon trees; and the country's largest bamboo collection. There's also a Native Plants and Native People trail.

8 Temecula Wine Country
MAP E1 ■ Thornton Winery: 32575 Rancho California Rd; 951 699 0099 ■ Callaway Vineyard & Winery: 32720 Rancho California Rd; 951 676 4001

During the mission days, Franciscan friars recognized that San Diego's soil and climate were ideal for planting grape vines. However, it wasn't until the 1960s that wine was first produced commercially. Now over two dozen wineries stretch across rolling hills studded with oak trees, most of them along Rancho

California Road. Wineries offer tastings for a small fee, and many of them operate restaurants and delis. Two of the most popular wineries in the area are Thornton Winery and Callaway Vineyard & Winery.

9 Rancho Santa Fe

This well-kept secret enclave, about 5 miles (8 km) east of the coast, harbors exquisite estates for the wealthy. Home to around 3,000 residents, The Covenant of Rancho Santa Fe was designated a California Historical Landmark as a historic planned community in 1989. Responsibility for this honor rests with architect Lillian Rice, who designed it in 1921. It is a lovely place to explore and dine in.

Luxurious living in Rancho Santa Fe

10 Mission Beach

MAP A4

The California beach scene struts in full glory along a narrow strip of land filled with vacation rentals and beachwear shops (see p49). Skaters, cyclists, and joggers whiz along the Strand, while surfers and sun worshipers pack the sand. Sometimes the streets become so crowded on the Fourth of July weekend that the police have to shut the area down. A block away, Belmont Park (see p59) is an old-fashioned fun zone with a vintage roller coaster.

Temecula Wine Country

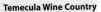

A MORNING IN LA JOLLA

> **MORNING**

Begin by looking out the front door of the landmark La Valencia Hotel (see p118). Turn left onto Prospect Street and walk past restaurants and art galleries. Before you reach Coast Boulevard, a stairway to the left leads to the Sunny Jim Cave, a fascinating, ocean-carved cave, named by L. Frank Baum (see p41). To the left of the entrance, a platform overlooks the caves. Continue along Coast Boulevard, admiring views of Torrey Pines and Scripps Pier. Pass through Ellen Browning Scripps Park (see p53). Beyond the end of the park is Children's Pool (see p58). Check out the seals and sea lions. Turn left on Cuvier Street and left onto Prospect Street. You'll now be at the Museum of Contemporary Art (see p34). Check out the exhibits or have a snack in the café. Louis Gill designed the original museum and the older architecture in this area. Walk back toward the village and peek inside 780 Prospect St; the cottage dates back to 1904. Cross Prospect at Fay but keep on Prospect. Pass through the Arcade Building to Girard Avenue. Turn right and window-shop along La Jolla's main street. Of note is Warwick's (7812 Girard Ave; La Jolla), a stationer and book-store, and R. B. Stevenson Gallery (7661 Girard Ave; La Jolla). Go north on Girard for a block and a half, and then finish your walk with one of the freshly baked delights at Girard Gourmet (see p105).

See map on p98

Coast Highway 101

 The Flower Fields
MAP D1 ■ 5704 Paseo del Norte, Carlsbad ■ Adm

In spring, the hillsides explode with blossoms of the giant tecolote ranunculus. The Carlsbad Ranch harvests 6–8 million bulbs for export.

2 LEGOLAND®
MAP D1 ■ 1 Legoland Dr, Carlsbad ■ 760 918 5346 ■ Adm

This theme park (see p58) is devoted to the plastic brick. Kids enjoy the hands-on activities and models, plus a waterpark and rides at THE LEGO® MOVIE™ World.

 Del Mar
MAP D2

The wealthiest community among North County's beach towns, Del Mar is filled with sidewalk cafés and shops.

4 Solana Beach
MAP D2

At this popular beach town, Cedros Design District shops and cafés are two blocks from Fletcher Cove; check with lifeguards before you swim.

 Cardiff-by-the-Sea
MAP D2

Surfers enjoy the reef break at Cardiff, while RV campers kick back at a beachside campground. The San Elijo Lagoon offers hiking trails through an ecological reserve.

San Diego Botanic Garden, Encinitas

 Leucadia
MAP D2

This sleepy town has a small beach and shops, restaurants, and galleries.

7 Carlsbad
MAP D1

In the 1880s, Captain John Frazier discovered that the water here had the same mineral content as a spa in Karlsbad, Bohemia. Today, this pretty village still draws visitors with its beaches, resorts, and shops.

 Oceanside
MAP D1 ■ California Surf Museum: 312 Pier View Way; 760 721 6876; open 10am–4pm daily; adm

Sandy beaches and a historic pier front this coastal town. The California Surf Museum shows a history of the sport.

9 Camp Pendleton
MAP D1

Endangered species and abundant wildlife thrive at the largest US Marine Corps base and amphibious training facility in the country.

10 Encinitas
MAP D2 ■ Self-Realization Fellowship Retreat and Hermitage: 215 W. K St ■ San Diego Botanic Garden: 230 Quail Gardens Dr; adm

Highlights here include the Self-Realization Fellowship Retreat and Hermitage, which has meditation gardens and a temple, and the San Diego Botanic Garden (see p100).

Shopping

① San Diego Botanic Garden Gift Shops

MAP D2 ▪ 230 Quail Gardens Dr, Encinitas ▪ 760 436 3036

Set in a public garden with more than 4,000 plant species from around the world, these shops sell unique home and garden decor, books, locally made jewelry and more. There's also a selection of plants, most propagated from species found in the garden.

A San Diego Botanic Garden shop

② REI

MAP C2 ▪ 5556 Copley Dr ▪ 858 279 4400

The go-to store for all your outdoor and sports needs, REI *(see p69)* also provides equipment rental for biking, camping, and more. In addition, it organizes activities such as full-moon hikes and offers rock-climbing lessons.

③ Chino

MAP D2 ▪ 6123 Calzada del Bosque, Rancho Santa Fe ▪ 858 756 3184

The Chino family farm and its store cater to famous chefs and lovers of superb fruit and vegetables.

④ Encinitas Seaside Bazaar

MAP D2 ▪ 459 South Coast Hwy 101, Encinitas ▪ 760 753 1611

This year-round open-air market offers unique antiques and home decor, arts and crafts, and various other delightful surprises.

⑤ Fresh Produce

MAP N2 ▪ 1147 Prospect St, La Jolla ▪ 858 456 8134

Colorful, comfy womenswear epitomizes the region's laid-back lifestyle. The pieces here flatter most shapes and sizes. Also stocked are bags, hats, and other seaside needs.

⑥ Trader Joe's

MAP A3 ▪ 1640 Garnet Ave, Pacific Beach ▪ 858 581 9101

This market sells imaginative salads, a wide variety of cheeses, wine, and fun ethnic food that you won't find in a regular supermarket.

⑦ Carlsbad Premium Outlets

MAP D1 ▪ 5620 Paseo del Norte, Carlsbad

Shop for bargains in one of the most pleasant outlet centers around. Gap, Bass, Salvatore Ferragamo, and Jones New York are all here.

⑧ Cedros Design District

MAP D2 ▪ Cedros Ave, Solana Beach

This former warehouse district has been transformed into a shopping street full of design stores, furnishings, and boutiques. The 100 shops at Cedros offer ethnic goods, clothing, and furniture.

⑨ Del Mar Plaza

MAP D2 ▪ 1555 Camino Del Mar, Del Mar

Italian home accessories, estate art, and well-known chains such as Banana Republic and White House/ Black Market can be found here.

⑩ Winery Gift Shops

MAP E1

Most wineries in Temecula operate gift shops that stock unusual cookbooks, entertaining supplies, and home decor items. Additionally, many have delis where you can find picnic food to accompany that bottle of wine you just bought.

See map on p98

Cafés and Bars

The palm-lined entrance to the Belly Up Tavern

1 Belly Up Tavern
MAP D2 ▪ 143 S. Cedros Ave,
Solana Beach ▪ 858 481 8140 ▪ Adm
One of the best live music venues
in the county. Old Quonset huts
have been acoustically altered to
showcase bands.

2 Encinitas Ale House
MAP D2 ▪ 1044 S. Coast Hwy
101, Encinitas ▪ 760 943 7180 ▪ $$
Popular for burgers and ales, this
cozy place has 32 taps rotating
Belgian and German beers, craft
beers, and international microbrews.

**3 Madeleine Cafe
& Bakery**
MAP D2 ▪ 240 S Cedros Ave, Solana
Beach ▪ 858 299 4788 ▪ $
Grab an outdoor table here and enjoy
classic French fare for a breakfast
treat or leisurely lunch.

4 Brockton Villa
MAP N2 ▪ 1235 Coast Blvd,
La Jolla ▪ 858 454 7393 ▪ $$
This historic place offers breakfast,
lunch, or dinner, and fabulous views.
Choices include seafood and steak.

5 Pannikin
MAP D2 ▪ 510 N. Coast Hwy
101, Encinitas ▪ 760 436 5824 ▪ $
Don't miss this coffeehouse located
inside a Santa Fe Railroad Depot. Sit
upstairs or outside on a shady deck.

**6 Living Room
Coffeehouse**
MAP N2 ▪ 1010 Prospect St ▪ 858
459 1187 ▪ $
Grab a back table at this hip
coffeehouse in upscale La Jolla
to enjoy a million-dollar view.

7 Ruby's Diner
MAP D1 ▪ 1 Oceanside Pier,
Oceanside ▪ 760 433 7829 ▪ $
Walk 1,942 ft (591 m) out to the pier's
end and order a salad or burger and
a malt at this 1940s-style diner.

8 VG Donut & Bakery
MAP D2 ▪ 106 Aberdeen Dr,
Cardiff ▪ 760 753 2400 ▪ $
This local favorite offers dozens of
variations of wedding cakes, pastries,
bear claws, bagels, fresh hot donuts,
cookies, and much more.

9 Lotus Café and Juice Bar
MAP D2 ▪ 765 S. Coast Hwy
101, Encinitas ▪ 760 479 1977 ▪ $
Lotus is especially appealing to
vegetarian and vegan diners, but
meat dishes are also offered.
Juices are freshly squeezed.

10 Lean and Green Café
MAP N3 ▪ 7825 Fay Ave,
Suite 180, La Jolla ▪ 858 459 5326 ▪ $
The organic offerings here include
wraps, salads, and smoothies, as
well as vegan and gluten-free items.

Places to Eat

1 **Del Mar Rendezvous**
MAP D2 ▪ 1555 Camino Del Mar, Suite 102, Del Mar ▪ 858 755 2669 ▪ Closed Thanksgiving Day & Super Bowl Sun ▪ $$
Book in advance for this popular modern Chinese restaurant, which also lists more than 100 wines.

2 **Poseidon**
MAP D2 ▪ 1670 Coast Blvd, Del Mar ▪ Closed Mon, Thanksgiving Day & Christmas ▪ 858 755 9345 ▪ $$
The beachside patio here is great for weekend brunch and cocktails at sunset.

3 **Eddie V's Prime Seafood**
MAP N2 ▪ 1270 Prospect St, La Jolla ▪ 858 459 5500 ▪ $$$
Fresh seafood and meat dishes (see p67) with views of La Jolla Cove, and there's live jazz nightly.

A plate of food at Eddie V's Prime Seafood

4 **101 Café**
MAP D1 ▪ 631 S. Coast Hwy, Oceanside ▪ 760 722 5220 ▪ $
Started as a roadside diner in 1928, 101 serves home-style comfort food.

5 **Emerald Chinese Seafood Restaurant**
MAP D3 ▪ 3709 Convoy St, Kearny Mesa ▪ 858 565 6888 ▪ $$
Favorites here (see p67) include crispy Peking duck and tender filet mignon.

6 **The Marine Room**
MAP P2 ▪ 2000 Spindrift Dr, La Jolla ▪ 858 459 7222 ▪ Closed Mon & Tue ▪ $$$
Elegant fine dining with beautiful surf and sunset views.

7 **Sushi Ota**
MAP B3 ▪ 4529 Mission Bay Dr ▪ 858 270 5670 ▪ $$
Considered the best spot for sushi in town, connoisseurs come to

---

PRICE CATEGORIES
Price categories include a three-course meal for one, half a bottle of wine, and all unavoidable extra charges including tax.

$ under $40 $$ $40–$80 $$$ over $80

Sushi Ota (see p66) for the day's freshest fish transformed into tasty works of art.

8 **Baci Ristorante**
MAP B3 ▪ 1955 W. Morena Blvd ▪ 619 275 2094 ▪ Closed Sun & Mon ▪ $$
Enjoy traditional veal, seafood, and pasta here (see p66), along with your choice of wine.

9 **Mille Fleurs**
MAP D2 ▪ 6009 Paseo Delicias, Rancho Santa Fe ▪ 858 756 3085 ▪ $$$
The most acclaimed restaurant in San Diego County provides a culinary feast. Fireplaces, fresh flowers, and tapestries complement the exquisite and beautifully presented food.

Elegant seating at Mille Fleurs

10 **Vigilucci's Cucina Italiana**
MAP D1 ▪ 2943 State St, Carlsbad ▪ 760 434 2500 ▪ $$
Classic antipasti, soups, and substantial servings of pastas and entrées are crowd-pleasers here, as is the daily happy hour.

See map on p98

Streetsmart

A cart displaying goods for sale
at the Old Town Market

Getting Around

Arriving by Air

San Diego International Airport (SAN), also known as Lindbergh Field, is only 3 miles (5 km) northwest of downtown San Diego. Domestic flights operate in and out of both Terminal 1 and Terminal 2; the latter also handles international carriers. The free Airport Loop shuttle bus connects the two terminals. The only non-stop international flights are to and from Canada, Mexico, Japan, Germany, and the UK.

Taxis and door-to-door shuttles may be found at the Transportation Plaza, accessible to Terminal 1 via a skybridge and to Terminal 2 directly across the street by exiting baggage claim. It's also possible to book a ride in advance with **SuperShuttle**.

Just outside baggage claim, bus route 992 takes about 10 minutes to reach downtown San Diego. It stops at the corner of W. Broadway and Kettner, which is directly across the street from the Santa Fe Depot (Amtrak and the Coaster) and America Plaza (trolley). Buses run every 15 minutes from 5am to 11:30pm on weekdays and every 30 minutes on weekends.

Tijuana International Airport is located 5 miles (8 km) east of downtown Tijuana, with frequent flights to the rest of Mexico, as well as direct flights to and from China and Japan. The **Cross Border Xpress**, a fee-based pedestrian bridge, allows passengers to cross the border between Mexico and the US with ease. On the US side, shuttles run by **Damaris Express Inc.** are available to take you to San Diego. Shuttles run approximately every two hours between 8:30am and 8:30pm, take 45 minutes to reach San Diego, and cost $13.

Arriving by Train

Amtrak's Pacific Surfliners arrive at the historic Santa Fe Depot, as does **Coaster**. About 11 trains travel daily to and from Orange County and Los Angeles, and several continue on to Santa Barbara.

Arriving by Road

Greyhound buses cover the entire US and most of Canada. There are direct connections from Los Angeles, with many continuing to the border and Tijuana's central bus terminal. A few daily buses go directly to Phoenix.

By car from Los Angeles, I-5 passes along coastal towns, heads into downtown, and continues to the international border at San Ysidro. Shortly before La Jolla, I-5 splits with I-805, reconnecting at the border. If driving from the east, I-8 passes through Mission Valley and ends just past SeaWorld. I-15 from Las Vegas serves inland San Diego County.

Arriving by Cruise Ship

All cruise ships moor at B Street Terminal along the Embarcadero on N. Harbor Drive within easy walking distance of downtown. Popular sailings include the Mexican Riviera or mini-cruises to Ensenada and Catalina.

Trains

A regional commuter rail service runs daily between the Santa Fe Depot and Oceanside. You can buy tickets at vending machines at stations and use them for 2 hours after purchase.

Buses and Trolleys

Public transport will take you just about anywhere in the city. The **San Diego Metropolitan Transit System** runs buses and trolleys. City buses connect with the **North County Transit District**, which serves coastal and inland San Diego County. Safety and hygiene measures, timetables, ticket information, transport maps, and more can be obtained from the websites of both transport providers. Inexpensive and fun, the red trolley is a light-rail system with three lines. The Blue line travels between the America Plaza downtown and the Mexican border at San Ysidro. The Green line is handy for the Gaslamp Quarter, the Convention Center, and Seaport Village. The Orange line crosses Downtown and continues out to El Cajon. Buses and trolleys operate from 4:30am until midnight.

You can only buy tickets on the bus with the exact change. Single adult fares are $2.50, except for express buses. Single adult trolley tickets are $2.50, valid for 2 hours. Vending machines sell trolley tickets at each stop. No transfers are allowed between buses and trolleys. If you plan to hop on and off buses and trolleys, 1-day and 30-day passes are available but only with a Compass Card. These reloadable cards may be purchased for $2 at The Transit Store and at Albertson's and Vons supermarkets.

Driving

You won't need a car in downtown San Diego, but it's essential to get around the rest of the city or region. A few car-rental agencies also have cars you can drive into Mexico, but you will need to agree this with your agent before traveling and buy additional insurance at the border. These include **Budget** and **California Baja Rent-a-Car**.

Taxis

Taxis don't cruise for fares. You can usually find a stand in front of large hotels, the airport, and some shopping centers. Rates are posted on the taxi door. You can also call **San Diego Taxi Company** for a ride. **Uber** services are popular, too.

Water Taxis

On-call **San Diego Water Taxis** will transport you to locations around the harbor. They run from Friday to Sunday, noon to 10pm.

Ferries

Flagship Cruises operates a service between San Diego and Coronado (see p15). Ferries depart from Broadway Pier at 990 N. Harbor Drive and the Convention Center Marina. From Coronado, ferries leave from the Coronado Ferry Landing, 1201 First Street. Ferries leave hourly from 9am to 9pm (to 10pm on Friday and Saturday). One-way fares are $5.

Walking

While many parts of San Diego are not particularly pedestrian-friendly, other areas are more walkable. Many neighborhoods in downtown San Diego are great places for a stroll, as is the island of Coronado, to the city's southwest. The reserves, parks, and preserves that surround the city also offer some excellent hiking and walking opportunities, including Mission Trails Regional Park (see p52).

Cycling

The greater San Diego region has over 1,300 miles (2,090 km) of bikeways. Bike rental shops such as **The Bike Revolution, Wheel Fun Rentals,** and **Stay Classy Bike Rentals** all offer good deals, as well as a variety of different types of bikes to hire.

DIRECTORY

ARRIVING BY AIR

Cross Border Xpress
W crossborderxpress.com/en/

Damaris Express Inc.
W damarisexpress.com

San Diego International Airport
W san.org

SuperShuttle
W supershuttle.com

Tijuana International Airport
W tijuana-airport.com

ARRIVING BY TRAIN

Amtrak
W amtrak.com

Coaster
W gonctd.com

ARRIVING BY ROAD

Greyhound
W greyhound.com

BUSES AND TROLLEYS

North County Transit District
W gonctd.com

San Diego Metropolitan Transit System
W sdmts.com

DRIVING

Budget
W budget.com

California Baja Rent-a-Car
W cabaja.com/usa-rentals

TAXIS

San Diego Taxi Company
C 619 566 6666

Uber
W uber.com

WATER TAXIS

San Diego Water Taxi
C 619 234 4111

FERRIES

Flagship Cruises
W flagshipsd.com/cruises/coronado-ferry

CYCLING

The Bike Revolution
W thebikerevolution.com

Stay Classy Bike Rentals
W stayclassybikes.com

Wheel Fun Rentals
W wheelfunrentals.com

Practical Information

Passports and Visas

For entry requirements, including visas, consult your nearest US embassy or check the website of the **US Department of State**.

All visitors to the US need a passport that is valid for at least six months from the date that they plan to enter the country. Citizens of 39 countries, including Australia, New Zealand, Chile, Japan, Singapore, South Korea, and the UK may enter without a visa under the Visa Waiver Program for stays of up to 90 days. To use this program, you must have an e-passport embedded with an electronic chip. You must also apply online for an Electronic System for Travel Authorization (**ESTA**) in advance of traveling.

Canadians must show a valid passport. Other foreign nationals need a valid passport and a tourist visa, obtainable from a US consulate or embassy in their home country. Having proof of a return ticket is also strongly recommended.

Government Advice

Now more than ever, it is important to consult both your and the US government's advice before travelling. The **UK Foreign and Commonwealth Office**, the US Department of State, and the **Australian Department of Foreign Affairs and Trade** offer the latest information on security, health and local regulations.

Customs Information

You can find information on the laws relating to goods and currency taken in or out of the US on the **US Customs and Border Protection** website.

If clearing customs and immigration at San Diego International Airport, the process is straightforward. If crossing at the San Ysidro International Border, expect long lines and additional scrutiny if you've come from the interior of Mexico.

Everyone above the age of 21 is allowed 1 liter of liquor and 200 cigarettes duty free. Citizens may bring in $400 worth of gifts; non-citizens, $100. Cash exceeding $10,000 must be declared. Fresh produce, meats, plants, and products from endangered species are prohibited.

Insurance

We recommend that you take out a comprehensive insurance policy covering theft, loss of belongings, medical care, cancellations and delays, and read the small print carefully.

Insurance is particularly important when travelling to San Diego as the cost of medical care is high everywhere in the US. If coming from abroad, check with your primary healthcare insurer at home to see if you have coverage while in the US.

If renting a car, establish what your auto insurer and credit card company covers in case of accident or theft. Otherwise, you may need to purchase additional collision damage and/or liability insurance. An auto insurance policy is not valid in Mexico; if you plan on driving there it's important to buy Mexican insurance before you cross over the border.

Health

The US has a world-class healthcare system. Payment of medical expenses is the patient's responsibility. It is therefore important to arrange comprehensive medical insurance before traveling.

For information regarding COVID-19 vaccination requirements, consult government advice.

San Diego has some of the best hospitals found in the country, including **Scripps Memorial Hospital La Jolla** and **Scripps Mercy Hospital** with 24-hr emergency rooms. If it is not a life-threatening situation, opt for urgent-care clinics which are less expensive. If you don't have health insurance, head to a community clinic. Expect to pay on the spot for services rendered. Many pharmacies in the city, such as Walgreens and CVS, are open 24 hours.

Enjoy the brilliant sunshine, but slather on the sunscreen during the day, and be sure to take a hat whenever you're outdoors.

The ocean waters to the city's west are generally clean, except after a heavy storm; then, accumulated and untreated runoff from miles away can wash down storm drains and empty into the ocean, and sewer leaks are common.

Smoking, Alcohol, and Drugs

You must be at least 21 years of age to drink or purchase alcohol, or to buy cigarettes and any other tobacco products throughout the US; expect to show photo ID even if you look much older. In California smoking is banned in all indoor public places, including restaurants, bars, and hotels, as well as in many outdoor public spaces, such as all parks, beaches, and pedestrian plazas. While US Federal law prohibits cannabis use, California has legalized limited amounts of 1 ounce (8g) for recreational use for anyone over the age of 21, including visitors. However, it is illegal to smoke cannabis in public places, including on public transport or in hotels or hostels. Taking any amount of cannabis across state lines or international borders is highly illegal, and would likely result in a jail sentence, as would being in possession of any other drug.

ID

There is no requirement for visitors to carry ID in San Diego, but due to occasional checks (especially at Federal sites) you may be asked to show a passport or other picture ID.

Personal Security

San Diego is a safe city; most petty crime is limited to theft and car break-ins. Common sense prevails: don't walk around late at night, and don't leave valuables inside your car. San Diego's proximity to the Mexican border makes car theft a concern – if your car is found across the border, the paperwork to bring it back is overwhelming. Take care to park in safe areas, such as lighted parking lots and garages with CCTV cameras and good security measures. If you have anything stolen, report the crime within 24 hours to the nearest police station and take ID with you. Get a copy of the crime report to make an insurance claim.

As in the rest of the US, dialing 911 in San Diego will put you in touch with the **emergency services**. Be prepared to specify your location and whether medical and/or police assistance is needed. Call the **San Diego Police** department for all other matters, including theft.

San Diego is a multicultural and diverse city, and locals are usually accepting of all people, regardless of their race, gender or sexuality. California recognized the rights of those wanting to legally change their gender in the mid-1980s and same-sex marriage was legalized in 2008. San Diego's Hillcrest neighborhood (see p86) is popular with the LGBTQ+ community; nearby is the **San Diego LGBT Community Center**, which offers advice and services. If you do feel unsafe, the **Safe Space Alliance** pinpoints your nearest place of refuge.

Dangerous riptides can occur along San Diego's coastal beaches; ask lifeguards about swimming conditions at unfamiliar beaches. Posted green flags indicate safe swimming, yellow flags mean caution, and red flags denote hazardous surf. If you are caught in a riptide, let the current carry you down the coast until it dies out, then swim in to the shore.

DIRECTORY

PASSPORTS AND VISAS

ESTA
🌐 esta.cbp.dhs.gov

US Department of State
🌐 travel.state.gov

GOVERNMENT ADVICE

Australian Department of Foreign Affairs and Trade
🌐 smartraveller.gov.au

UK Foreign and Commonwealth Office
🌐 gov.uk/foreign-travel-advice

CUSTOMS INFORMATION

US Customs and Border Protection
🌐 cbp.gov

HEALTH

Scripps Memorial Hospital La Jolla
📞 858 457 4123

Scripps Mercy Hospital
📞 619 294 8111

PERSONAL SECURITY

Emergency Services
📞 911

Safe Space Alliance
🌐 safespacealliance.com

San Diego LGBT Community Center
🌐 thecentersd.org

San Diego Police
📞 619 531 2000

Travelers with Specific Requirements

The **San Diego Tourism Authority** lists a number of resources and links to services for visitors with disabilities on their website. These include transportation assistance, sightseeing tours, wheelchair beach access, shows with subtitles for the hearing impaired, braille guides at museums and attractions, hotel and dining facilities, and more. **AccessibleGO** is another good planning resource for attractions, hotels, equipment rental, and itineraries in the city.

Many sights in San Diego cater to those with specific requirements. Audio tours, tour scripts, subtitled films, wheelchairs, and other facilities are available at attractions such as the USS Midway Museum *(see p16)* and the Fleet Science Center *(see p58)*, among others. American Sign Language interpreters are available (call in advance) at the Museum of Photographic Arts *(see p20)*, the San Diego Zoo Safari Park *(see p99)*, and Seaworld *(see p99)*. The San Diego Zoo *(see p19)*, meanwhile, has scooter and wheelchair rentals as well as Braille guides.

All buses, trolleys, and the Coaster are equipped with lifts. Amtrak trains have limited accessible spaces and recommend advance reservations. Greyhound provides a lift-equipped bus with advance notice. Super Shuttle *(see p108)* provides transportation from the airport, also with advance notice.

If driving your own car, reserved parking spaces are marked by a blue curb, a blue-and-white wheelchair logo on the pavement, and by a posted sign. You may park for free in most metered areas, but a special permit must be displayed.

Every intersection and sidewalk in San Diego has ramped curbs or at least a ramped driveway. Ramped access is standard in government buildings, museums, some theaters, and large hotels and restaurants.

Hotels with more than five rooms must provide accessible accommodation. It is best to call in advance to reserve one of these rooms, and specify if you need a roll-in shower. When making restaurant reservations, do clarify that you require access.

Imperial Beach, Ocean Beach, Coronado, Mission Beach, Oceanside, Silver Strand State Beach, and La Jolla Shores have power and manual beach chairs. These are free to use, but book ahead.

Time Zone

From the first Sunday in November until the second Sunday in March, San Diego operates on Pacific Standard Time (PST), which is 8 hours behind Greenwich Mean Time (GMT). For the remaining months, the clock moves ahead 1 hour and becomes Pacific Daylight Time (PDT), or 7 hours behind Greenwich Mean Time.

Money

The currency in San Diego is the US dollar. If paying for anything in cash with a merchant, expect to have any paper bills larger than a $20 scrutinized.

San Diego International Airport has international exchange kiosks in Terminal 1 and Terminal 2. Travelex has two other locations in Horton Plaza and Fashion Valley. Major banks handle most transactions, but you will need to bring ID. Large hotels exchange currency as well, but offer low rates. Exchange windows in San Ysidro handle transactions in dollars and pesos.

There are 24-hour ATMs all over the city. ATMs inside convenience stores or malls charge you for use, as does your own bank if you go outside the network. Most major banks are found throughout San Diego. Banking hours are usually 9am or 10am until 6pm, Monday through Friday, with Saturday hours from 9am to 1pm or 2pm.

Major credit and debit cards, including American Express, are widely accepted in San Diego, as are prepaid currency cards and Apple Pay. Contactless payments are becoming increasingly common throughout the city.

If using buses in San Diego, be aware that you can only purchase tickets on the bus with the exact change. Ticket machines for buses are cash only.

Tipping is the norm in the US. In restaurants it is normal to tip 15–20 per cent of the total bill. Allow for a tip of 15 per cent for taxi drivers and bar staff. Hotel porters and housekeeping expect $1–$2 per bag or day.

Electrical Appliances

The US uses plugs with two flat blades and sometimes a third round grounding pin. Either type will fit in American sockets. Power is set at 110 volts, so 220-volt-only appliances will not work efficiently, and a power converter will be necessary.

If you are coming from abroad, you will need a plug adapter. It might be easier to purchase this before you travel, as most adapters sold in US stores are just for Americans traveling abroad. If you forget to bring an adapter, you can usually find one in a Best Buy store.

Mobile Phones and Wi-Fi

If you carry an unlocked phone, you can find SIM cards with a variety of prepaid, no-contract plans at supermarkets, corner stores, Target, and Walmart. T-Mobile and AT&T stores also carry SIM cards.

There are free Wi-Fi hotspots all over the city: in cafés, fast-food restaurants, and even in Horton Plaza shopping center. Public libraries also have computer terminals to use, as do hostels, but you must be a guest. Most hotels offer free Wi-Fi, as does San Diego International Airport (but in 30-minute sessions).

Postal Services

Regular post office hours are 8:30am–5pm Monday to Friday, with some branches open on Saturday mornings. Stamps are usually available from vending machines in the lobby, and signage indicates the cost of postage for mail sent to domestic and international addresses. Stamps are available at many supermarkets and franchised mail service stores, which also provide shipping services. Hotel concierges can post mail for you. FedEx and UPS offer courier services with guaranteed overnight delivery and reliable international service. Many of their franchise offices sell packaging supplies. Much cheaper, the US Postal Service offers overnight service in the continental US and two- and three-day services internationally.

Weather

San Diego enjoys the most temperate climate in the nation. The rainy season usually begins in December, with a few large storms rolling in by spring. Winter days can be warm and sunny, but ocean temperatures are cold. Late spring often presents what locals call "May gray" and "June gloom." During this time, you often find a lot of low cloud cover, but you can just as easily get endless days of dazzling sunshine. Sometimes you might find a rare, mild summer shower. Summer evenings are pleasant but often cool, so make sure you bring a sweater or lightweight jacket with you. During the summer months, be aware that if you leave the coast and head inland the temperatures are considerably warmer.

Opening Hours

COVID-19 Increased rates of infection may result in temporary opening hours and/or closures. Always check ahead before visiting museums, attractions and hospitality venues.

Most museums are open from 10am to 5pm. However, check the website or call before making plans, as many tend to close one day of the week.

Retail shops usually open at 10am and close at 5pm or 6pm. Regular hours at shopping malls are 10am–9pm Mon–Sat and 11am–7pm Sun. Department stores sometimes open at 7am for super-sales or extend their hours during the holiday season. Malls close only during a few major holidays, such as Christmas and New Year; however, some stores may be open on Thanksgiving (the fourth Thursday in November) and Easter Sunday.

You shouldn't have any trouble finding 24-hour convenience stores, gas stations, drug stores, and supermarkets. A few Walmarts and Targets in San Diego are also open 24 hours.

Visitor Information

The website of the **San Diego Tourism Authority**, the country's official tourist organization, offers comprehensive information for visitors to the city. You'll also find download links for various mobile apps, including for some of San Diego's main attractions, as well as for areas such as La Jolla (see pp34–5) and Little Italy (see p78). Once you're in San Diego, stop by the **San Diego Visitor Information Center** at the Embarcadero, where staff will answer your questions about activities and tours. They also sell tickets to attractions. The **Coronado Visitor Center** can give you a map of Coronado and suggest activities in the area.

Go City passes offer up to 50 per cent off most attractions in San Diego. There's also **CityPASS**, which offers discounts to attractions in San Diego and Southern California.

Language

English is the official language in San Diego. However, the city also contains a large Spanish-speaking population, thanks to its proximity to the Mexican border. You may often hear Spanish being spoken, and see signs in both English and Spanish. Many people in the city are bilingual.

Taxes and Refunds

The current sales tax in the majority of San Diego County is 7.75 per cent. Since none of these taxes are levied at a national level, tourists cannot claim sales tax refunds.

Trips and Tours

Old Town Trolley Tours makes 11 stops in a continuous 2-hour loop around San Diego's most popular attractions, including Old Town, the Embarcadero, Seaport Village, Gaslamp Quarter, Balboa Park, Coronado, and Little Italy. From Old Town, tours depart at 9am and every 30 minutes until late afternoon, depending on the time of year. Departure times vary from each stop. The tours are narrated and drivers are quite knowledgeable. Adult tickets are $44 ($41.80 online), and you can hop on and hop off as you please. The same company operates San Diego SEAL tours, which uses a type of amphibious vehicle to first tour the streets of the city before it enters San Diego Bay to power past Navy vessels and harbor sights, and La Jolla and Mission Beach tours.

Five Star Tours operates bus tours to popular attractions throughout San Diego County, including Legoland, San Diego Safari Park, wine tours, city tours, and a number of trips to Tijuana and Ensenada, Mexico.

San Diego Ride & Tours offers half- and full-day narrated tours on air-conditioned buses or mini-buses around San Diego, the harbor, and Temecula Wine Country.

Flagship Cruises (see p109) offers several ways to tour the harbor. There are 1- and 2-hour narrated trips covering the harbor, Shelter Island, Point Loma, Coronado Bridge, and more. Dinner, nature, and whale-watching cruises are also available.

Walking tours – like those organized by **Balboa Park Tours** and **Coronado Walking Tour** – are also very popular.

Shopping

You don't have to go far to find something to buy in San Diego. Shopping malls are everywhere, with the same stores as other malls in the country. The best bargains can be found around public holidays. San Diego has three major outlet centers within an hour's driving distance: the **Carlsbad Premium Outlets** in North County, the **Las Americas Premium Outlets** at San Ysidro, and **Viejas Outlet Center** on the Viejas Reservation, east on I-8. You can usually find good deals at the designer spin-off shops. Upscale boutiques are located in La Jolla, and if you're looking for unusual gifts, the museum shops in Balboa Park (see p82) are a good starting point. A non-refundable sales tax of 7.75 per cent is added to all retail purchases.

Dining

With its proximity to the Pacific Ocean, Mexico, and surrounding ranch and farmlands, you won't go hungry in San Diego. The Gaslamp Quarter is packed with restaurants, but many can get busy and rather noisy. Foodies tend to go to restaurants in Little Italy or Bankers Hill. For romantic dining with an ocean view, La Jolla offers the city's best choices. You'll find a variety of cuisines on offer throughout the city, with a wealth of options in the Hillcrest neighborhood. The best family-friendly restaurants are in Mission Valley and Mission Bay.

On weekends throughout the year and during the summer months, it's wise to make a reservation. Lunch hours are usually 11am to 2pm or 3pm, with dinner service beginning at 5pm or 5:30pm and kitchens closing at 10pm. Dress codes tend to be casual in most places. Most food servers expect a 15–20 per cent tip; leave it in cash, or add it to your credit card bill. With large parties, an 18–20 percent gratuity may be automatically added to the check. Entrées on the lunch menu are often less than half the price of those at dinner. Some restaurants

offer early-bird dinners from 4pm until 6pm, with a limited number of discounted entrées. Many restaurants and bars offer happy hours on weekdays. For the price of a drink and a few dollars, you can snack on anything from a hot buffet to chips and dip. Some Mexican restaurants sell inexpensive tacos on "Taco Tuesdays." Check out the advertisements in the *San Diego Reader*.

The legal drinking age in California is 21. If you look under 30, restaurant servers and merchants will ask to see your photo ID, so take it with you when dining out. Note that in Tijuana, the legal drinking age is 18.

Accommodations

Home to everything from ultra-posh hotels to humble dormitory-style hostels, San Diego offers accommodations for every budget. Given the

city's popularity, be sure to make your reservations early to avoid frustration.

Staying at a motel chain like **Days Inn** or **Motel 6** offers standardized accommodations with no surprises. Most major chains can be found in Mission Valley's Hotel Circle. Parking is generally free, breakfast is often provided, and there are usually no unexpected fees.

If you plan to stay in San Diego for more than a few weeks, consider renting an apartment. Keep in mind that summer rentals, especially along the beach, are more costly. Be sure to ask what amenities are included.

The only comfortable place to camp legally near the city is in **San Diego Metro KOA**. This well-located spot offers a swimming pool, hot tub, and bicycle rentals. RV owners can try **Campland on the Bay**, which also accepts tent campers.

DIRECTORY

Places to Stay

PRICE CATEGORIES

For a standard, double room per night (with breakfast if included), taxes, and extra charges.

$ under $200 $$ $200–$300 $$$ over $300

Luxury Hotels

Hard Rock Hotel

MAP K6 ■ 207 5th Ave ■ 619 702 3000 ■ www. hardrockhotelsd.com ■ $

The contemporary rooms and suites at this hotel look out across the Gaslamp Quarter. The atmosphere is lively, and friendly staff will cater to your needs, even loaning you a Fender guitar. Enjoy a drink at the rooftop lounge or taste the impeccable food at Nobu, the on-site restaurant.

Coronado Island Marriott Resort and Spa

MAP C6 ■ 2000 2nd St, Coronado ■ 619 435 3000 ■ www.marriott.com/ sanci ■ $$

Lush grounds with a relaxed feel, and dedicated staff make this hotel a top choice. Californian and French styling prevails, with some rooms looking out across the bay to San Diego. The hotel also runs a watertaxi service.

Estancia La Jolla Hotel & Spa

MAP A1 9700 N. Torrey Pines Rd ■ 855 318 7602 ■ www.meritagecollection. com/estancia-la-jolla ■ $$

Elegant rooms offer luxury and comfort in this Spanish ranch-style hotel surrounded by lush gardens. Indulge yourself at the spa or heated salt-water pool. A short walk leads down to the beach.

La Casa del Zorro Resort & Spa

MAP F2 ■ 3845 Yaqui Pass Rd, Borrego Springs ■ 760 767 0100 ■ www. lacasadelzorro.com ■ $$

This classic desert resort offers poolside rooms and private casitas, featuring wood-burning fireplaces and marble bathtubs. Facilities include a spa, fitness center, three swimming pools, and tennis courts. Conditions for stargazing in the desert sky are perfect.

L'Auberge Del Mar Resort & Spa

MAP D2 ■ 1540 Camino del Mar, Del Mar ■ 858 386 1336 ■ www.lauberge delmar.com ■ $$

Join the list of Hollywood notables who relax at this boutique hotel and spa near the Pacific. The rooms have marble baths and many include private balconies and fireplaces.

Rancho Bernardo Inn

MAP E2 ■ 17550 Bernardo Oaks Dr, Rancho Bernardo ■ 888 976 4417 ■ www.ranchobernardo inn.com ■ $$

Bougainvillea-adorned patios and red-tile-roof adobe buildings evoke images of early California at this relaxing resort set in stunning grounds. Life here revolves around the adjoining golf course, spa, and tennis courts.

Solamar

MAP K5 ■ 435 6th Ave ■ 619 819 9500 ■ www. hotelsolamar.com ■ $$

This boutique hotel offers a complimentary wine hour every evening in the fireplace lounge. California cuisine features at the JSix restaurant, and the fourth-floor pool deck with the Upper East rooftop bar and fire pits is popular with the locals, too.

The Westgate Hotel

MAP J4 ■ 1055 Second Ave ■ 619 238 1818 ■ www.westgatehotel. com ■ $$

With a lobby that suggests the anteroom of the Palace of Versailles, complete with Baccarat crystal chandeliers and French tapestries, this grand hotel offers good value for its location. Spacious rooms with European decor have city views.

Fairmont Grand Del Mar

MAP E2 ■ 5300 Grand Del Mar Court ■ 858 314 2000 ■ www.fairmont.com/ san-diego ■ $$$

Discover San Diego's inland beauty at this Spanish- and Italian-style destination resort. Luxurious rooms with fine amenities, superb service, golf, pools, spa, hiking trails, and equestrian facilities are reasons never to leave.

Four Seasons Residence Club Aviara

MAP D2 ■ 7210 Blue Heron Place ■ 760 603 3700 ■ www.fourseasons. com/privateretreats ■ $$$

With impeccable service and a superb setting, this

property offers luxurious residential rentals. Choose between indoor and outdoor treatment rooms, or a suite with a whirlpool.

The Lodge at Torrey Pines

MAP D2 ▪ 11480 N. Torrey Pines Rd, La Jolla ▪ 858 453 4420 ▪ www.lodge torreypines.com ▪ $$$
Located on the cliffs of Torrey Pines, this lodge offers exquisite accommodations. The rooms look out onto a courtyard that reflects the surrounding coastal environment and the greens of the Torrey Pines Golf Course. Early California Impressionist art graces the walls and signature restaurant.

Rancho Valencia Resort

MAP E2 ▪ 5921 Valencia Circle, Rancho Santa Fe ▪ 858 756 1123 ▪ www. ranchovalencia.com ▪ $$$
Bougainvillea cascades over the Spanish casitas in this stunning resort. Many rooms feature cathedral ceilings, private terraces, and fireplaces. Rejuvenation treatments include reflexology, aromatherapy, and various massages.

Historic Hotels

The Cosmopolitan Hotel

MAP N5 ▪ 2660 Calhoun St ▪ 619 297 1874 ▪ www. oldtowncosmopolitan. com/hotel ▪ $
Built as a family home in 1827, this hotel features Victorian-style bedrooms and baths, furnished with antiques. Maintaining the style, rooms have Wi-Fi, but no TVs or telephones.

A breakfast of home-made pastries is served in the saloon.

Gaslamp Plaza Suites

MAP K4 ▪ 520 E St ▪ 619 232 9500 ▪ www. gaslampplaza.com ▪ $
Now on the National Register of Historic Places, this building still features much of its original 1913 craftsmanship, such as Australian gumwood, Corinthian marble, and an elevator door made of brass. Complimentary breakfast is served on the rooftop terrace.

Inn at the Park

MAP C5 ▪ 525 Spruce St ▪ 619 291 0999 ▪ No air conditioning ▪ www.shell hospitality.com ▪ $
This 1926 inn was popular with Hollywood celebrities en route to their vacations in Mexico in the 1920s and 1930s. The original fixtures lend a delightful retro touch.

Glorietta Bay Inn

MAP C6 ▪ 1630 Glorietta Blvd, Coronado ▪ 619 435 3101 ▪ www.gloriettabay inn.com ▪ $$
Many of the original fixtures of John D. Spreckels' *(see p41)* 1908 Edwardian mansion remain, including the unique hand-made plaster moldings, chandeliers, and a marble staircase. Splurge on one of the antique-filled guest rooms inside the house for a more decadent experience.

The Grande Colonial

MAP N3 ▪ 910 Prospect St, La Jolla ▪ 888 828 5498 ▪ www.thegrande colonial.com ▪ $$
La Jolla's first hotel was designed by Spanish

Revival architect Richard Requa *(see p41)*. The 1913 building houses luxury suites, while a 1926 building contains the main hotel. Elegantly appointed rooms are in keeping with the hotel's European ambience.

Horton Grand Hotel

MAP J5 ▪ 311 Island Ave ▪ 619 544 1886 ▪ www.hortongrand. com ▪ $$
Rebuilt from two Victorian-era hotels, this hotel reflects the character of the Gaslamp Quarter. Rooms are individually decorated in period style, and each has a gas fireplace.

The Inn at Rancho Santa Fe

MAP E2 ▪ 5951 Linea del Cielo, Rancho Santa Fe ▪ 858 756 1131 ▪ www.theinnatrsf. com ▪ $$
Refined elegance distinguishes this romantic country inn. Many of the red-roofed adobe casitas scattered about the lush grounds boast comfy queen-sized beds, fireplaces, and kitchens.

La Jolla Beach and Tennis Club

MAP N3 ▪ 2000 Spindrift Dr ▪ La Jolla ▪ 858 412 0721 ▪ www.ljbtc.com ▪ $$$
This resort is perfect for an active family: guests can choose to ocean swim, kayak, play tennis or golf, or simply enjoy the sunshine. You can step out the door onto a pristine sand beach. Rooms with kitchenettes are available.

La Valencia Hotel
MAP N2 ▪ 1132 Prospect St, La Jolla ▪ 855 476 6870 ▪ www.lavalencia. com ▪ $$$
Since 1926, La Valencia has enchanted with its splendid Mediterranean ambience, exquisite decor, and ideal location on the cliffs above La Jolla Cove. Rooms vary from quite small to large ocean villas.

U.S. Grant
MAP J4 ▪ 326 Broadway ▪ 619 232 3121 ▪ www. marriott.com ▪ $$$
Ulysses S. Grant Jr. commissioned this stately 1910 Renaissance palace. Set in the historic Gaslamp Quarter, it retains its timeless elegance with mahogany furniture and paneling, tile floors, and luxurious rooms.

Spa Hotels

Omni La Costa Resort & Spa
MAP D1 ▪ 2100 Costa Del Mar Rd, Carlsbad ▪ 760 438 9111 ▪ www.omni hotels.com/hotels/san-diego-la-costa ▪ $$
This Spanish-Colonial complex contains two PGA championship golf courses, a tennis center, several restaurants, and a spa and fitness center offering several health and beauty treatments.

Cal-a-Vie
MAP D1 ▪ 29402 Spa Havens Rd, Vista ▪ 888 373 8773 ▪ www.cal-a-vie.com ▪ $$$
Exhilarating programs focus on fitness, nutrition, and personal care. The Mediterranean-style villas provide luxurious accommodations (packages for 3–7 nights only).

Golden Door
MAP E2 ▪ 777 Deer Springs Rd, San Marcos ▪ 760 744 5777 ▪ www. goldendoor.com ▪ $$$
Modeled after the ancient ryokan inns, Japanese gardens, streams, and waterfalls make a glorious backdrop to a week of fitness and meditation. For most of the year, the spa is a women-only domain.

Rancho La Puerta
MAP F3 ▪ 476 Tecate Rd, Tecate, Baja California, Mexico ▪ 858 764 5500 ▪ www.rancholapuerta. com ▪ $$$
Since 1940, guests have pursued body and mind fitness at this beautiful Mexican-Colonial-style resort. Lodgings are in casitas decorated with folk art and bright fabrics. The dining room specializes in homegrown organic food.

Business Hotels

Town & Country Resort Hotel
MAP C4 ▪ 500 Hotel Circle N. ▪ 619 291 7131 ▪ www. towncountry.com ▪ $
This sprawling family-owned resort has an onsite convention center and 1,000 rooms. Next door is a golf course, a trolley stop, and the Fashion Valley Mall.

Embassy Suites Hotel San Diego Bay – Downtown
MAP H5 ▪ 601 Pacific Hwy ▪ 619 239 2400 ▪ www. embassysuites.com ▪ $$
Guests enjoy spacious suites that have a living area and a separate bedroom. All rooms open onto a palm-tree-filled atrium and offer a view of the bay or city. Enjoy a dip in the indoor pool.

Hilton La Jolla Torrey Pines
MAP D2 ▪ 10950 N. Torrey Pines Rd, La Jolla ▪ 858 558 1500 ▪ www.hiltonla jollatorreypines.com ▪ $$
This low-key but chic hotel is located next to the Torrey Pines Golf Course. A valet looks after your immediate needs, and a car service can drive you to La Jolla. All rooms have balconies or terraces, and many feature ocean or harbor views.

Hyatt Regency La Jolla
MAP B1 ▪ 3777 La Jolla Village Dr, La Jolla ▪ 858 552 1234 ▪ www.lajolla. hyatt.com ▪ $$
Postmodern architect Michael Graves designed this Italian-style palace hotel. A fitness spa and highly acclaimed restaurants are situated next door. Corporate guests can access the business center.

Omni San Diego Hotel
MAP K6 ▪ 675 L St ▪ 619 231 6664 ▪ www.omni hotels.com ▪ $$
A skyway links the hotel to Petco Park, and you can even see the ball field from some rooms. Comfy rooms sport great bathrooms, and if you must tend to business, the Convention Center is only a few blocks away.

Manchester Grand Hyatt San Diego
MAP H5 ▪ 1 Market Place ▪ 619 232 1234 ▪ www.manchester grand.hyatt.com ▪ $$$
Two high-rise towers hold 1,625 rooms, many

with personal work areas and all with high-speed Internet. The lounge on the 40th floor is one of San Diego's best. Guests can also make use of two rooftop pools and the 24-hour fitness center.

Marriott Marquis San Diego Marina

MAP J6 ■ 333 W. Harbor Dr ■ 619 234 1500 ■ www.marriotthotels. com ■ $$$
Most rooms at this hotel are set up with worktables and high-speed Internet, offering scenic views of the waterfront and San Diego Bay. The marina and waterfall swimming pool make great distractions.

Westin Gaslamp Quarter San Diego

MAP J4 ■ 910 Broadway Circle ■ 619 239 2200 ■ www.marriott.com ■ $$$
Attached to the Horton Plaza Park, this down-town hotel is close to restaurants and entertain-ment venues. It offers a range of event and meeting spaces, a workout room, and swimming pool. The Gaslamp Quarter and Convention Center are within walking distance.

Westin San Diego Downtown

MAP H4 ■ 400 W. Broad-way ■ 619 239 4500 ■ www.marriott.com/ hotels/travel/sanws-the-westin-san-diego-downtown/ ■ $$$
You can't miss this hotel's green silhouette of glass towers. Amenities include ergonomic work chairs and high-speed Internet access. The Convention Center is within easy walking distance.

Mid-Range Hotels

Bay Club Hotel & Marina

MAP B5 ■ 2131 Shelter Island Dr ■ 619 224 8888 ■ www.bayclub hotel.com ■ $
Rattan furniture and tropical fabrics give a Polynesian cast to this hotel. The best rooms are at the back and have views of the marina and Point Loma. Breakfast is included.

Crowne Plaza San Diego

MAP Q4 ■ 2270 Hotel Circle N. ■ 619 297 1101 ■ www. cp-sandiego.com ■ $
In the 1960s, a wave of Polynesian-themed hotels sprang up in the area, and those that survived now have a trendy retro feel to them. The tropical decor still rules the public areas, but the rooms are contem-porary and overlook the pool or nearby golf course.

The Dana on Mission Bay

MAP B4 ■ 1710 W. Mission Bay Dr ■ 619 222 6440 ■ www.thedana.com ■ $
This hotel is incredibly popular with families. All the water activities of Mission Bay are close by, and the hotel also has on-site watersports and bike rentals. Tropical landscaping surrounds the grounds, and the swimming pool is a real hit with kids.

Humphrey's Half Moon Inn and Suites

MAP B5 ■ 2303 Shelter Island Dr ■ 619 224 3411 ■ www.halfmooninn.com ■ $
Its summer concert series (see p60), tropical landscaping, private marina, and long list of activities make this hotel an ideal choice for those looking for some enter-tainment. You can pay a little more for a room with a view of the bay.

Best Western Plus Hacienda Hotel Old Town

MAP P5 ■ 4041 Harney St ■ 619 298 4707 ■ www. bestwestern.com ■ $$
On a hillside overlooking Old Town, this charming hacienda-style hotel offers rooms that have private balconies or look onto a courtyard. Free airport transportation is provided.

Hotel Indigo

MAP K5 ■ 509 9th Ave ■ 619 727 4000 ■ www. hotelindigo.com ■ $$
Rooms at this trendy, pet-friendly boutique hotel in the Gaslamp Quarter come with plush bedding, hardwood floors, and complimentary Internet access. The bar terrace looks right over Petco Park and has spectacular views of the city skyline.

Waterfront Hotels

Bahia Resort Hotel

MAP A4 ■ 998 W. Mission Bay Dr ■ 858 488 0551 ■ www.bahiahotel.com ■ $$
This venerable Mission Bay Hotel is right next to the bay and Mission Beach. Among the facil-ities on offer are tennis courts, a hydro-therapy pool, and a fitness center. At night, you can enjoy live music on the *Bahia Belle*, a stern-wheeler that floats on the bay every evening.

For a key to hotel price categories see p116

Carlsbad Inn Beach Resort

MAP D1 ▪ 3075 Carlsbad Blvd, Carlsbad ▪ 760 434 7020 ▪ www.carlsbad inn.com ▪ $$

Families really love this sprawling resort. Its rooms and timeshare condominiums are available nightly or weekly. Several activities and classes are held daily, and there is also a good Mexican restaurant.

Catamaran Resort Hotel and Spa

MAP A3 ▪ 3999 Mission Blvd ▪ 858 488 1081 ▪ www.catamaranresort. com ▪ $$

This Polynesian-themed hotel offers a long list of water activities. It is within walking distance of many restaurants, and Tiki torches light your way through lushly lands-caped grounds. The upper floors of the towers have great views.

Hyatt Regency Mission Bay Spa and Marina

MAP B4 ▪ 1441 Quivira Rd ▪ 619 224 1234 ▪ www.missionbay. regency.hyatt.com ▪ $$

This large, family-friendly resort offers pools and water slides, as well as access to a full marina with kayaks, jet-skis, and sailboats. Spacious rooms feature balconies with lovely views of the Pacific, Mission Bay, or the lush gardens.

Pacific Terrace

MAP A3 ▪ 610 Diamond St ▪ 858 581 3500 ▪ www. pacificterrace.com ▪ $$

Sunset views over the Pacific define high living at one of San Diego's finest beach hotels. Large guest rooms come with a balcony or patio. There is no full-service restaurant, but the friendly staff can suggest neighborhood dining options.

Sea Harbor Hotel

MAP B5 ▪ 1325 Scott St ▪ 619 224 3371 ▪ www. seaharborhotel.com ▪ $$

This waterside hotel at the Point Loma Marina is well situated for sportfishing activities and the Cabrillo National Monument. Along with the stylish rooms, guests can enjoy the huge outdoor swimming pool and on-site parking.

Crystal Pier Hotel & Cottages

MAP A3 ▪ 4500 Ocean Blvd ▪ 800 748 5894 ▪ www.crystalpier.com ▪ $$$

Reservations are essential for these 1927 Cape Cod-style cottages that sit directly on the pier. Many have kitchenettes, and patios with views of Pacific Beach.

Tower 23 Hotel

MAP A3 ▪ 723 Felspar St, Pacific Beach ▪ 858 270 2323 ▪ www.t23hotel. com ▪ $$$

Situated right on the Pacific Beach, this stylish hotel features luxury rooms with rain showers, sleek teak furnishings, and high-end amenities. In-room massages are available on request. The classy JRDN restaurant serves delicious authentic Californian seafood.

Bed and Breakfasts

Hillcrest House

MAP C4 ▪ 3845 Front St ▪ 619 990 2441 ▪ www.hillcresthouse.net ▪ $

Choose from five uniquely decorated rooms at this vintage bed and breakfast. It is well situated for San Diego's attractions, and hostess Ann can help you plan your day over a healthy continental breakfast or in the parlor in front of the fireplace.

Julian Gold Rush Hotel

MAP E2 ▪ 2032 Main St, Julian ▪ 760 765 0201 ▪ www.julianhotel.com ▪ $

Built in 1897 by a freed enslaved person, this quaint inn is the oldest continually operating hotel in Southern California. The rooms and cottages are furnished with antiques and vintage decor, and the breakfasts are exceptional.

The Artists' Loft

MAP E2 ▪ Strawberry Hill, Julian ▪ 760 765 0765 ▪ No air conditioning ▪ www.artistsloft.com ▪ $$

Three secluded cabins deep in the woods will inspire the artist within you. Airy Craftsman-style interiors feature natural wood, fine textiles, a full kitchen, and a wood-burning stove. From your screened porch, gaze at stunning distant views.

Beach Hut Bed & Breakfast

MAP B3 ▪ 3761 Riviera Dr ▪ 858 272 6131 ▪ www. beachhutbb.com ▪ $$

Relax around the landscaped patio and

small pool at this quiet B&B on Sail Bay in Mission Bay Park. The spacious Tuscan room and garden cottage are beautifully styled, with every comfort.

Hotel Marisol

MAP C6 ▪ 1017 Park Place , Coronado ▪ 619 365 4677 ▪ www.marisolcoronado. com ▪ $$

Escape the crowds at this intimate Spanish-style inn, which has hosted guests since 1927. Guest rooms are decorated in soft colors and have shutters. A continental breakfast is complimentary, as are beach chairs and bicycles. Coronado's famous beach is only 5 minutes away.

The Inn at Europa Village

MAP E1 ▪ 33350 La Serena Way, Temecula ▪ 951 506 1818 ▪ www. europavillage.com ▪ $$
Ideally situated for touring the Temecula vineyards, rooms in this Mission-style inn have private balconies, Jacuzzis, and fireplaces. Rates include a scrumptious continental breakfast with fresh pastries.

Orchard Hill Country Inn

MAP F2 ▪ 2502 Washington St, Julian ▪ 760 765 1700 ▪ www. orchardhill.com ▪ $$
At this most luxurious of Julian's B&B inns, you can stay in a Craftsman-style cottage with a whirlpool tub, a fireplace, and a private porch. The tasty breakfasts make for a good start to the day.

Budget Hotels and Hostels

Apple Tree Inn

MAP E2 ▪ 4360 Highway 78, Julian ▪ 760 765 0222 ▪ www.julianapple treeinn.com ▪ $
A few miles outside of Julian, this small cinder-block-style motel offers a quiet night's sleep in basic but tidy rooms that have mountain views and an outdoor pool. Hiking trails, a few restaurants, and shops are nearby. Pet-friendly.

Borrego Springs Motel

MAP F1 ▪ 2376 Borrego Springs Rd ▪ 760 767 4339 ▪ www.borrego springsmotel.com ▪ $
There are seven queen-bed rooms and one twin-bed room in this no-frills but sparkling clean motel – perfect for those who want to enjoy the surrounding desert. Despite solar power, the motel offers no Wi-Fi, TV, or tele-phones. The helpful proprietors, who live onsite, are local experts.

HI San Diego Downtown Hostel

MAP K5 ▪ 521 Market St ▪ 619 525 1531 ▪ www. hihostels.com/hostels/ hi-san-diego-downtown ▪ $
This bright hostel offers dorm rooms and a few private rooms, some with baths. There is also free airport transportation and breakfast, along with kitchen and lounge facilities, laundry service, and Internet access. The hostel organizes free tours and events that guests can utilize.

Kings Inn

MAP C4 ▪ 1333 Hotel Circle S. ▪ 619 297 2231 ▪ www.kingsinnsan diego.com ▪ $
This vintage-style inn with a swimming pool and spa tub has clean, comfortable rooms and friendly, helpful staff. Good onsite restaurants serve breakfast, lunch, and dinner.

La Pensione

MAP H3 ▪ 606 W. Date St ▪ 619 236 8000 ▪ www. lapensionehotel.com ▪ $
In the heart of Little Italy, La Pensione offers boutique rooms with a queen-size bed as well as a pretty courtyard, excellent spa, and free coffee and pastry at the café. Some of the city's best Italian restaurants are a stone's throw away.

Old Town Inn

MAP B4 ▪ 4444 Pacific Hwy ▪ 619 260 8024 ▪ www.oldtown-inn. com ▪ $
The rooms here are clean and comfy, and the hotel offers one of the better breakfasts around. An efficiency unit comes with a microwave, refrig-erator, and range top, and parking is also free.

USA Hostels Gaslamp

MAP K5 ▪ 726 5th Ave ▪ 619 278 9748 ▪ No private bathrooms ▪ www.usahostels.com ▪ $
A popular centrally located hostel offering dorm rooms and some private rooms. Facilities include a free continental breakfast, lockers with charging outlets, a laundry, kitchen, and lounge.

For a key to hotel price categories see p116

General Index

Acknowledgments

This edition updated by

Contributor Donna Dailey
Senior Editor Alison McGill
Project Editors Parnika Bagla, Rachel Laidler
Project Art Editor Ankita Sharma
Editor Chhavi Nagpal
Picture Research Administrator Vagisha Pushp
Picture Research Manager Taiyaba Khatoon
Publishing Assistant Halima Mohammed
Jacket Designer Jordan Lambley
Senior Cartographer Subhashree Bharati
Cartography Manager Suresh Kumar
Senior Production Editor Jason Little
Senior Production Controller
Samantha Cross
Deputy Managing Editor Beverly Smart
Managing Editors Shikha Kulkarni,
Hollie Teague
Managing Art Editor Sarah Snelling
Senior Managing Art Editor Priyanka Thakur
Art Director Maxine Pedliham
Publishing Director Georgina Dee

DK would like to thank the following for
their contribution to the previous editions:
Mary Barrus, Pamela Barrus, Hilary Bird,
Roger Devenyns, Marael Johnson

The publisher would like to thank the
following for their kind permission to
reproduce their photographs:

Key: a-above; b-below/bottom; c-center; f-far;
l-left; r-right; t-top

123RF.com: Florian Blümm 10cl; Kan
Khampanya 4crb; Stephen Minkler 11tl;
Sean Pavone 4b.

Alamy Stock Photo: America 3tr, 10bl, 106–7; Art
Directors & TRIP 95cl; Paul Briden 16cla; Citizen
of the Planet 32cla, 49cl; Collection Christophel
61tr; Richard Cummins 67tr; Ian G Dagnall 45cl,
77tl, 100cla; David R. Frazier Photolibrary, Inc.
24cr; Danita Delimont 79cl, 94t; f8grapher 16br;
GALA Images 10c; Joseph S Giacalone 33tl, 49b,
94clb; Ian Dagnall Commercial Collection 12br;
69cra; Images-USA 7br; Blaine Harrington III
21bl; Juice Images 54bl; David Kilpatrick 73br;
Elizabeth Leyden 30bc; LH Images 27tl, 71tr; W.
G. Murray 63cl; Natura-Light 35tl; PhotoBliss
4clb; George Ostertag 98tl, 102b; RooM the
Agency 36cl; Science History Images 40b;
SeBuKi 55cl; Steve Shuey 37tl; Witold Skrypczak
17crb; Stephen Saks Photography 70t;
Sueddeutsche Zeitung Photo 41cl; SuperStock
31tl; Craig Steven Thrasher 93bl; TongRo
Images 57cb; Visions from Earth 12–3; Nik
Wheeler 25crb, 30clb; Richard Wong 96cl; ZUMA
Press Inc 17cl, 27bc, 56br, 73cla, 89cla, 101cl.

AWL Images: Danita Delimont Stock 2tl, 8–9;
Marco Simoni 28–9c.

Balboa Park Conservancy: 46tl.

Belly Up Tavern: Pixel Perfect Images/
Daniel Knighton 104tl.

Belmont Park: 32–3, 59b.

Bertrand at Mr. A's: 66t.

Cafe Sevilla: 62br.

The Cottage: 65tr.

Crest Cafe: 89cb.

Del Mar Rendezvous: 105ca.

Dreamstime.com: Adeliepenguin 34–5, 100–1;
Agezinder 44bl; Americanspirit 93tr; Joe Avery
56tl; Rinus Baak 78tl; Jay Beiler 30–31; Jon
Bilous 3tl, 44tr, 74–5, 90–1; Scott Burns 31crb;
Alan Crosthwaite 26cb; Kobby Dagan 18crb, 72bl;
Dobino 72c; Durson Services Inc. 11cr;
F11photo 10cla, 80crb; Sandra Foyt 52tl; Ben
Graham 29cr, 48tl; Hannator92 50-51; Hellen8
26–7c; Irina88w 84tr, 86cl; Ritu Jethani 19crb,
68bl, 88clb; Kongomonkey 7tl, 42cla; Chon Kit
Leong 35crb; Meunierd 77crb; Stephen Minkler
40ca; Susanne Neal 58tl; Saletomic 1; Sean
Pavone 4cla; Petthomas 14–5; Photoquest 52bl;
Razyph 72tr; Gino Rigucci 92ca; Stasvolik 54tr;
Steveheap 42br; Mirko Vitali 53tr; Welcomia
45tr; Angie Westre 55br.

Eddie V's Prime Seafood: 67clb.

The Field Irish Pub: 64b.

Getty Images: Davel5957 4cl; Blaine Harrington
III 4t; Mark Whitt Photography 99b; Sam
Antonio Photography 1; Stephen Saks 36bl;
Stringer / Robert Benson 13crb; Maureen P
Sullivan 32bc; Rob Tilley 4cr.

Humphrey's Concerts by the Bay: 60b.

iStockphoto.com: Siestacia 85cr; Ron Thomas
11cra, 11crb, 11b, 15tc, 28br, 36–7c, 86–7;
Tobiasjo 28cl; Art Wager 80tl.

La Jolla Playhouse: Kevin Berne 34bl;
Joan Marcus 2tr, Sutton Foster (center)
and the cast of La Jolla Playhouse's Tony
Award-winning production of, THOROUGHLY
MODERN MILLIE 38–9.

Lestat's Coffee House: 64ca.

Lou & Mickey's: 83cr.

Manchester Grand Hyatt: 65cl.

Maritime Museum of San Diego: 15crb, 47cla.

Miguel's Cocina: 97b.

Mille Fleurs: 105crb.

Museum of Man: 76tl.

Museum of Photographic Arts: RyanGobuty
Gensler 82cr.

The Old Globe: 60cla.

Photoshot: 13tl; Nikhilesh Haval 25cl.

Prohibition: 62tl.

**Putnam Foundation, Timken Museum of Art,
San Diego:** 70bc.

Reuben H. Fleet Science Center: 18cla.

Rex by Shutterstock: Everett Collection 41tr.

San Diego Automotive Museum: 21c.

San Diego Botanic Garden: 103cla.

San Diego Museum of Art: 20clb, 82tl.

San Diego Natural History Museum: 20tr.

Seaport Village: 14br, 69b.

Spanish Village Art Center: 47b.

Spin: 63tr.

Spreckels Organ Pavilion: Michael Cox 18–9c, Robert Lang 71cl.

Spreckels Theatre: 61cl.

SuperStock: AGE Fotostock/George Ostertag 53cl; Richard Cummins 43br; George Ostertag 99cra.

Vocabulary: 81b.

Cover

Front and spine: **Dreamstime.com:** Saletomic.

Back: **Dreamstime.com:** Saletomic b; **Getty Images:** Stone / David Madison tl; **iStockphoto. com:** f11photo crb, Mindy_Nicole_Photography cla, Ron Thomas tr.

Pull Out Map Cover

Dreamstime.com: Saletomic.

All other images © Dorling Kindersley
For further information see:
www.dkimages.com

Penguin
Random
House

First edition 2005

First published in Great Britain
by Dorling Kindersley Limited,
DK, One Embassy Gardens, 8 Viaduct
Gardens, London SW11 7BW, UK

The authorised representative in the EEA is
Dorling Kindersley Verlag GmbH. Arnulfstr.
124, 80636 Munich, Germany

Published in the United States by
DK Publishing, 1745 Broadway, 20th Floor,
New York, NY 10019, USA

Copyright © 2005, 2022 Dorling
Kindersley Limited
A Penguin Random House Company

22 23 24 25 10 9 8 7 6 5 4 3 2 1

A CIP catalog record is available
from the British Library.

A catalog record for this book is available
from the Library of Congress.

ISSN: 1479 344X

ISBN: 978-0-2415-5929-1

Printed and bound in China

www.dk.com

*As a guide to abbreviations in visitor information
blocks:* **Adm** = admission charge; **D** = dinner.

MIX
Paper from
responsible sources
FSC™ C018179

This book was made with Forest
Stewardship Council ™ certified
paper – one small step in DK's
commitment to a sustainable future.
For more information go to
www.dk.com/our-green-pledge

Street Index